At Issue

Is Iran a Threat to Global Security?

Stefan Kiesbye, Book Editor

GREENHAVEN PRESS
A part of Gale, Cengage Learning

GALE
CENGAGE Learning

Detroit • New York • San Francisco • New Haven, Conn • Waterville, Maine • London

Christine Nasso, *Publisher*
Elizabeth Des Chenes, *Managing Editor*

© 2010 Greenhaven Press, a part of Gale, Cengage Learning.

Gale and Greenhaven Press are registered trademarks used herein under license.

For more information, contact:
Greenhaven Press
27500 Drake Rd.
Farmington Hills, MI 48331-3535
Or you can visit our Internet site at gale.cengage.com

For product information and technology assistance, contact us at

Gale Customer Support, 1-800-877-4253
For permission to use material from this text or product, submit all requests online at www.cengage.com/permissions

Further permissions questions can be e-mailed to permissionrequest@cengage.com

Articles in Greenhaven Press anthologies are often edited for length to meet page requirements. In addition, original titles of these works are changed to clearly present the main thesis and to explicitly indicate the author's opinion. Every effort is made to ensure that Greenhaven Press accurately reflects the original intent of the authors. Every effort has been made to trace the owners of copyrighted material.

Cover image © Images.com/Corbis.

LIBRARY OF CONGRESS CATALOGING-IN-PUBLICATION DATA

Is Iran a threat to global security? / Stefan Kiesbye, book editor.
   p. cm. -- (At issue)
   Includes bibliographical references and index.
   ISBN 978-0-7377-4667-9 (hardcover) -- ISBN 978-0-7377-4668-6 (pbk.)
   1. Iran--Military policy. 2. Nuclear weapons--Iran. 3. Iran--Foreign relations--1997- 4. Security, International. 5. World politics--21st century. I. Kiesbye, Stefan.
   UA853.I7I76 2010
   355'.033055--dc22
                                                                2009042501

Printed in the United States of America
1 2 3 4 5 6 7 14 13 12 11 10

Contents

Introduction

In his 2002 State of the Union address, President Bush included Iran in his now infamous Axis of Evil, together with Iraq and North Korea. Many nations are worried about the nuclear program Iran is pursuing, and about nuclear weapons being built in a country whose president Mahmoud Ahmadinejad has often embraced a controversial rhetoric. In his speech at Columbia University, in September 2007, he said through a translator, that he found it disheartening that no open discussion about the Holocaust was possible, and that any researcher who was approaching the topic with a skeptical attitude was in danger of being imprisoned. Ahmadinejad also asked, why, if the Holocaust was accepted as a reality, the Palestinian people had to pay the price for crimes that were not committed by them. The Holocaust took place in Europe, so why were Palestinians punished for it, he demanded to know. On the topic of Iran's nuclear program he said that his country is a member of International Atomic Energy Agency, and has been for over 33 years. Ahmadinejad claimed that the by-law of the agency guarantees all member states the right to use nuclear energy for peaceful purposes. Therefore he deemed Iran's nuclear program lawful and in compliance with international treaties.

But the current debate about nuclear proliferation and human rights violations in Iran overlooks the long history the United States has had with Iran, a history that is marred by manipulation, the backing of dictatorial regimes, and siding with its enemy Iraq during the Iran-Iraq War. Starting in the 1950s, the United States aggressively sought to alter Iranian domestic and foreign politics. As actor Sean Penn writes in the *San Francisco Chronicle* on August 22, 2005:

> Just after the midpoint of the 20th century, Prime Minister Muhammad Mussadiq—erudite, secular and committed to a

7

democratic vision of Iran—cast a formidable shadow across the world stage. At home his popularity grew as he insisted on putting an end to Britain's long-standing plunder of Iranian oil. In April 1951, Mussadiq took decisive action, nationalizing the British oil firm that had enjoyed a sweetheart deal with Iran's government. Despite fury in London, he set up the National Iranian Oil Co. British leaders got nowhere when they asked the Truman administration to use the U.S. government's more trusted position in Tehran to help overthrow Mussadiq.

But when Dwight Eisenhower became president in 1953, according to Penn:

> his foreign-policy team rolled up its spooky sleeves to get the job done. The regal Shah of Iran—a faithful buddy of British oil executives—was losing his power struggle with Mussadiq, and in August the Shah abruptly left the country and fled to Rome. The CIA ... quickly moved to subvert Iranian democracy. CIA operative Kermit Roosevelt, a grandson of Theodore Roosevelt, labored feverishly in Tehran to coordinate a coup that brought down Mussadiq in August 1953 and quickly restored the Shah to the throne. Western oil companies were back in charge of Iran's oil, and the Shah initiated what turned out to be a quarter-century of political repression, torture, and killing.

The Shah, Mohammad Reza Shah Pahlavi, continued to receive significant American support and was often a guest in Washington. (In 2000, U.S. Secretary of State Madeleine Albright apologized for U.S. involvement in the coup and for U.S. support of the brutal dictatorial regime of the Shah, which repressed political dissent.) In 1977, President Jimmy Carter openly criticized the Shah's government and its violations of human rights. He demanded that the Shah relax restrictions upon free speech and allow the voices of political dissidents to be heard.

Two years later, the Iranian Revolution overthrew the Shah and replaced him with Ayatollah Ruholla Khomeini, the Supreme Leader. The revolution came as a shock to the United States; not even the CIA had anticipated it. When President Carter allowed the Shah U.S. entry to be treated for cancer, radical students stormed the American Embassy in Tehran. Fifty-two U.S. diplomats were held hostage for more than a year. "You have no right to complain, because you took our whole country hostage in 1953," said one of the hostage takers to Bruce Laingen, chief U.S. diplomat in Iran at the time, as Stephen Kinzer states on *Democracy Now* on March 3, 2008. The April 24, 1980, American attempt to free the hostages—Operation Eagle Claw—was aborted and caused the death of eight American soldiers. The United States broke off diplomatic relations with Iran, and they have not been restored since.

In September 1980, Iraq invaded Iran and the ensuing war lasted for eight years. The United States backed Iraq and its leader Saddam Hussein, and, under President Ronald Reagan, supplied the country with intelligence and economic aid. It also provided heavily armored civilian vehicles, which could be used for military purposes. When the U.S. shot down an Iranian civilian airliner toward the end of the war in 1988, killing 290 people from six nations, among them many children, the relations between the two countries reached a new low.

Sanctions and embargoes have isolated Iran, which is currently seeking a larger role on the international stage. *At Issue: Is Iran a Threat To Global Security?* explores the multifaceted perspectives of this pressing issue.

1

Iran Has Instigated a New Cold War

Thomas Friedman

Thomas Friedman has won the Pulitzer Prize three times as a reporter for the New York Times *and as a commentator. His most recent book is* The World is Flat: A Brief History of the 21st Century.

There is a Cold War. America's opponent is no longer Russia, however, but Iran. America's approach to diplomacy and military action has eroded the respect of other nations, and it is more despised than feared or loved. The only way to deal with Iran is to give the country incentives to stop its nuclear ambitions and pressure its regime to stop supplying militants in the region with money and weapons. A military confrontation is not an option.

The next American president will inherit many foreign policy challenges, but surely one of the biggest will be the cold war. Yes, the next president is going to be a cold-war president—but this cold war is with Iran.

That is the real umbrella story in the Middle East today—the struggle for influence across the region, with America and its Sunni Arab allies (and Israel) versus Iran, Syria and their non-state allies, Hamas [a Palestinian, sociopolitical, militant Sunni movement] and Hezbollah [a Shia Islamist political and paramilitary organization based in Lebanon]. As the May 11 [2008] editorial in the Iranian daily *Kayhan* put it, "In the power struggle in the Middle East, there are only two sides: Iran and the U.S."

For now, Team America is losing on just about every front. How come? The short answer is that Iran is smart and ruthless, America is dumb and weak, and the Sunni Arab world is feckless and divided. Any other questions?

The outrage of the week [in May 2008] is the Iranian-Syrian-Hezbollah attempt to take over Lebanon. Hezbollah thugs pushed into Sunni neighborhoods in West Beirut, focusing particular attention on crushing progressive news outlets like Future TV, so Hezbollah's propaganda machine could dominate the airwaves. The Shiite militia Hezbollah emerged supposedly to protect Lebanon from Israel. Having done that, it has now turned around and sold Lebanon to Syria and Iran.

Iran Has Gained Influence

All of this is part of what Ehud Yaari, one of Israel's best Middle East watchers, calls "Pax Iranica." In his April 28 column in *The Jerusalem Report,* Mr. Yaari pointed out the web of influence that Iran has built around the Middle East—from the sway it has over Iraq's prime minister, Nuri Kamal al-Maliki, to its ability to manipulate virtually all the Shiite militias in Iraq, to its building up of Hezbollah into a force—with 40,000 rockets—that can control Lebanon and threaten Israel should it think of striking Tehran, to its ability to strengthen Hamas in Gaza and block any U.S.-sponsored Israeli-Palestinian peace.

For now, Team America is losing on just about every front.

"Simply put," noted Mr. Yaari, "Tehran has created a situation in which anyone who wants to attack its atomic facilities will have to take into account that this will lead to bitter fighting" on the Lebanese, Palestinian, Iraqi and Persian Gulf fronts. That is a sophisticated strategy of deterrence.

The [President George W.] Bush team, by contrast, in eight years has managed to put America in the unique position in the Middle East where it is "not liked, not feared and not respected," writes Aaron David Miller, a former Mideast negotiator under both Republican and Democratic administrations, in his provocative new book on the peace process, titled *The Much Too Promised Land*.

"We stumbled for eight years under [President] Bill Clinton over how to make peace in the Middle East, and then we stumbled for eight years under Bush over how to make war there," said Mr. Miller, and the result is "an America that is trapped in a region which it cannot fix and it cannot abandon."

Look at the last few months [before May 2008], he said: President Bush went to the Middle East in January, Secretary of State Condoleezza Rice went in February, Vice President Dick Cheney went in March, the secretary of state went again in April, and the president is there again this week. After all that, oil prices are as high as ever and peace prospects as low as ever. As Mr. Miller puts it, America right now "cannot defeat, co-opt or contain" any of the key players in the region.

We Americans are not going to war with Iran, nor should we.

America Needs Leverage

The big debate between [2008 Democratic presidential candidates] Barack Obama and Hillary Clinton is over whether or not the United States should talk to Iran. Obama is in favor; Clinton has been against. Alas, the right question for the next president isn't whether we talk or don't talk. It's whether we have leverage or don't have leverage.

When you have leverage, talk. When you don't have leverage, get some—by creating economic, diplomatic or military incentives and pressures that the other side finds too tempting or frightening to ignore. That is where the Bush team has been so incompetent vis-a-vis Iran.

The only weaker party is the Sunni Arab world, which is either so drunk on oil it thinks it can buy its way out of any Iranian challenge or is so divided it can't make a fist to protect its own interests—or both. We Americans are not going to war with Iran, nor should we. But it is sad to see America and its Arab friends so weak they can't prevent one of the last corners of decency, pluralism and openness in the Arab world from being snuffed out by Iran and Syria. The only thing that gives me succor is the knowledge that anyone who has ever tried to dominate Lebanon alone—Maronites [a Christian sect], Palestinians, Syrians, Israelis—has triggered a backlash and failed.

"Lebanon is not a place anyone can control without a consensus, without bringing everybody in," said the Lebanese columnist Michael Young. "Lebanon has been a graveyard for people with grand projects." In the Middle East, he added, your enemies always seem to "find a way of joining together and suddenly making things very difficult for you."

2

American Double Standards Provoke Iran's Antagonism

Stephen Zunes

Stephen Zunes is a professor of politics at the University of San Francisco, and the author of Tinderbox: U.S. Middle East Policy and the Roots of Terrorism.

The difficulty with diplomatic efforts involving Iran and the United States is that both views are heavily influenced by a fundamentalist doctrine of good versus evil, and that both parties tend toward hypocrisy and double standards. Furthermore, Iran has been unfairly singled out by the United States as a threat to global security. The dialogue between the countries should not be based on hype and inflammatory rhetoric.

This past Wednesday [September 26, 2007], I was among a group of American religious leaders and scholars who met with Iranian president Mahmoud Ahmadinejad in New York. In what was billed as an inter-faith dialogue, we frankly shared our strong opposition to certain Iranian government policies and provocative statements made by the Iranian president. At the same time, we avoided the insulting language employed by Columbia University president Lee Bollinger before a public audience two days earlier.

The Iranian president was quite unimpressive. Indeed, with his ramblings and the superficiality of his analysis, he came across as more pathetic than evil.

Stephen Zunes, "My Meeting with Ahmadinejad," *Foreign Policy In Focus*, September 28, 2007. Copyright © 2007 Institute for Policy Studies. Reproduced by permission.

The more respectful posture of our group that morning

The more respectful posture of our group that morning led to a more open exchange of views. Before an audience largely composed of Christian clergy, he reminded us that we worship the same God, have been inspired by many of the same prophets, and share similar values of peace, justice, and reconciliation. The Iranian president impressed me as someone sincerely devout in his religious faith, yet rather superficial in his understanding and inclined to twist his faith tradition in ways to correspond with his pre-conceived ideological positions. He was rather evasive when it came to specific questions and was not terribly coherent, relying more on platitudes than analysis, and would tend to get his facts wrong. In short, he reminded me in many respects of our president [George W. Bush].

A Narrow Perspective

Both Ahmadinejad and George W. Bush have used their fundamentalist interpretations of their faith traditions to place the world in a Manichean [a former major Iranian gnostic religion] perspective of good versus evil. The certitude of their positions regardless of evidence to the contrary, their sense that they are part of a divine mission, and their largely successful manipulation of their devoutly religious constituents have put these two nations on a dangerous confrontational course.

Ahmadinejad can get away with it because he is president of a theocratic political system that allows very limited freedoms and opportunities for public debate. We have no such excuse here in the United States, however, for the strong bipartisan support for Bush's righteous anti-Iranian crusade, most recently illustrated by a series of provocative anti-Iranian measures recently passed by an overwhelming margin of the Democratic-controlled Congress.

There are many differences between the two men, of course. Perhaps the most significant is that, unlike George W. Bush, Ahmadinejad has very little political power, particularly in the areas of military and foreign policy. So why, given Ahmadinejad's lack of real political power, was so much made of his annual trip to the opening session of the UN [United Nations] General Assembly?

Both Ahmadinejad and George W. Bush have used their fundamentalist interpretations of their faith traditions to place the world in a . . . perspective of good versus evil.

Ahmadinejad's Political Weakness

The president of Iran is constitutionally weak. The real power in Iran lies in the hands of Ayatollah Khamenei and other conservative Shiite clerics on the Council of Guardians. Just as they were able to stifle the reformist agenda of Ahmadinejad's immediate predecessor Mohammed Khatami, they have similarly thwarted the radical agenda of the current president, whom they view as something of a loose cannon.

Furthermore, Ahmadinejad's influence is waning. The new head of the Revolutionary Guard Ali Jafari is from a conservative sub-faction opposed to the more radical elements allied with Ahmadinejad. He replaced the former Guard head Yahya Rahim-Safavi, who was apparently seen as too openly sympathetic to the president. In addition, former president and Ahmadinejad rival Ayatollah Rafsanjani was recently elected to head the powerful experts' assembly, defeating Ayatollah Ahmad Jannati, who was backed by Ahmadinejad supporters and other hardliners.

Ahmadinejad's election in 2005 was not evidence of a turn to the right by the Iranian electorate. The clerical leadership's restrictions on who could run made it nearly impossible for any real reformist to emerge as a presidential contender.

Ahmadinejad's opponent in the runoff election was the 70-year-old Ayatollah Rafsanjani, who was seen as a corrupt representative of the political establishment. The fact that he had become a millionaire while in government overshadowed his modest reform agenda. By contrast, Ahmadinejad, the relatively young Tehran mayor, focused on the plight of the poor and cleaning up corruption.

Under Ahmadinejad's leadership, the level of corruption and the economic situation for most Iranians has actually worsened.

As a result, Iranian voters were forced to choose between two flawed candidates. The relatively liberal contender came across as an out-of-touch elitist, and his ultraconservative opponent was able to assemble a coalition of rural, less-educated, and fundamentalist voters to conduct a pseudo-populist campaign based on promoting morality and value-centered leadership. In short, it bore some resemblance to the presidential election in the United States one year earlier.

Waning Popularity

Under Ahmadinejad's leadership, the level of corruption and the economic situation for most Iranians has actually worsened. As a result, in addition to losing the backing of the clerical leadership, he has lost much of his base and his popularity has plummeted. In municipal elections last December [2006], Ahmadinejad's slates lost heavily to moderate conservatives and reformers. Why, then, is all this attention being given to a relatively powerless lame duck president of a Third World country?

Part of the reason may be that highlighting Ahmadinejad's extremist views and questioning his mental stability helps convince millions of Americans that if [the Iranians develop] an atomic bomb, [they] will immediately use it against the

United States or an ally such as Israel. With more than 200 nuclear weapons and advanced missile capabilities, Israel has more than enough deterrent capability to prevent an Iranian attack. Obviously, American deterrent capabilities are even greater. However, if you depict Iran's leader as crazy, it puts nuclear deterrence in question and helps create an excuse for the United States or Israel to launch a preventive war prior to Iran developing a nuclear weapons capability.

In reality, though, the Iranian president is not commander-in-chief of the armed forces, so Ahmadinejad would be incapable of ordering an attack on Israel even if Iran had the means to do so. Though the clerics certainly take hard-line positions on a number of policy areas, collective leadership normally mitigates impulsive actions such as launching a war of aggression. Indeed, bold and risky policies rarely come out of committees.

Focusing on Ahmadinejad's transparent double standards and hypocrisy makes it easier to ignore similar tendencies by the U.S. president.

It should also be noted that while Ahmadinejad is certainly very anti-Israel, his views are not as extreme as they have been depicted. For example, Ahmadinejad never actually threatened to "wipe Israel off the map" nor has he demonstrated a newly hostile Iranian posture toward the Jewish state. Not only was this oft-quoted statement a mistranslation—the idiom does not exist in Farsi and the reference was to the dissolution of the regime, not the physical destruction of the nation—the Iranian president was quoting from a statement by Ayatollah Khomeini from over 20 years earlier. In addition, he explicitly told our group on September 26 [2007] that there was "no military solution to the Israeli-Palestinian conflict" and that it was "not Iran's intention to destroy Israel."

The Saddam Niche

The emphasis and even exaggeration of Ahmadinejad's more bizarre and provocative statements makes it easier to ignore his more sensible observations, such as: "Arrogant power seekers and militarists betray God's will." It also makes it politically easier for the United States to refuse to engage in dialogue or enter into negotiations, such as those that led to an end of Libya's nuclear program in 2003. Ahmadinejad has welcomed American religious delegations to Iran, but the United States has denied visas to Iranian religious delegations to this country. The Bush administration has also blocked cultural and scholarly exchanges.

The disproportionate media coverage of Ahmadinejad's UN visit also suggests that Ahmadinejad fills a certain niche in the American psyche formerly filled by the likes of [U.S.-deposed leader of Iraq] Saddam Hussein and [Libyan leader] Muammar Qaddafi as the Middle Eastern leader we most love to hate. It gives us a sense of righteous superiority to compare ourselves to these seemingly irrational and fanatical foreign despots. If these despots can be inflated into far greater threats than they actually are, these threats can justify the enormous financial and human costs of maintaining American armed forces in that volatile region to protect ourselves and our allies and even to make war against far-off nations in "self-defense." Such inflated threats also have the added bonus of silencing critics of America's overly-militarized Middle East policy, since anyone who dares to challenge the hyperbole and exaggerated claims regarding these leaders' misdeeds or to provide a more balanced and realistic assessment of the actual threat they represent can then be depicted as naive apologists for dangerous fanatics who threaten our national security.

Double Standards on Human Rights

Furthermore, focusing on Ahmadinejad's transparent double standards and hypocrisy makes it easier to ignore similar tendencies by the U.S. president. Ahmadinejad's speech at the UN on September 25 [2007] was widely criticized for its emphasis on human rights abuses by Israel and the United States while avoiding mention of his own country's poor human rights record. It helps distract attention from President Bush's speech that same day, in which he criticized human rights abuses by dictatorial governments in Belarus, North Korea, Syria, Iran, Burma, and Cuba, but avoided mentioning human rights abuses by Egypt, Saudi Arabia, Equatorial Guinea, Oman, Pakistan, Cameroon, and Chad, or any other dictatorship allied with the United States.

> *We focus on Iranian human rights abuses while we continue to support the even more oppressive and theocratic Islamic regime in Saudi Arabia.*

The outreach by Christian clergy to Ahmadinejad, whom the *New York Times* described as "the religious president of a religious nation who relishes speaking on a religious plane," came out of a belief in the importance of dialogue and reconciliation. Our group emphasized that we were critical of the U.S. government's threats, but also raised concerns on such issues as Iranian human rights abuses and Ahmadinejad's hostility toward Israel and denial of the Holocaust. Virtually all our questions, however, were thrown back in criticisms toward the United States. "Who are the ones that are filling their arsenals with nuclear weapons?" he said. "The United States has developed a fifth generation of atomic bombs and missiles that could hit Iran. Who is the real danger here?"

Indeed, it must seem odd to most people in the Middle East that the United States, which is 10,000 miles away from the longest-range weapon the Iranians can currently muster and possesses by far the most powerful military apparatus the world has ever seen, is depicting Iran as the biggest threat to its national security. As Ahmadinejad put it to our group that morning, "The United States has many thousands of troops on our borders and threatens to attack us. Why is it, then, that Iran is seen as a threat?" And though most Iranians, Arabs, and other Muslims recognize Ahmadinejad as an extremist, he is unfortunately correct in accusing the United States of unfairly singling out Iran, an issue that has real resonance in that part of the world.

America's Obsession with Iran

Indeed, the United States is obsessed with Iran's nuclear program—still many years away from producing an atomic bomb—while we support the neighboring states of Pakistan, India, and Israel, which have already developed nuclear weapons and which are also in violation of UN Security Council resolutions regarding their nuclear programs. We blame Iran for the deaths of American soldiers in Iraq, yet 95% of U.S. casualties are from anti-Iranian Sunni insurgents. We focus on Iranian human rights abuses while we continue to support the even more oppressive and theocratic Islamic regime in Saudi Arabia. We attack the Iranian president's denial of the genocide of European Jews while remaining silent in the face of Turkish leaders' denial of the genocide of Armenians. One of the most important principles of most faith traditions is moral consistency. Few receive greater wrath in most holy texts than hypocrites.

Americans have many legitimate concerns regarding Iranian policies in general and the statements of President Ahmadinejad in particular. However, as long as U.S. policy appears to be based upon such opportunistic double standards rather than consistent principles, Ahmadinejad's inflammatory rhetoric will continue to find an audience.

3

Iran Is Behind Conflict in the Middle East

Michael Ledeen

Michael Ledeen is Freedom Scholar at the Foundation for the Defense of Democracies.

Disruption in the Middle East is often being portrayed as a conflict of Israel with its neighbors. The real problems are neither Syria nor Lebanon, however, but Iran, which gives money and support to terrorist groups such as Hamas and Hezbollah. Despite sectarian differences and violence in other parts of the Middle East, the Shia Iranians are helping Shia and Sunni insurgents to cause turmoil and upheaval. Since Israel cannot afford to wage war against Iran, it must hope for its Western allies to recognize the real threat and take steps to thwart it.

Everyone in the Middle East knows that the serious component of the Battle of Gaza is all about Iran. The Egyptian president, Hosni Mubarak, recently warned that Iran is trying to "devour" the Arab world. Mohammed Abdallah Al Zulfa, of the Saudi Arabian Shura Council, reminded [television channel] Alhurra's viewers that "Iran is the big threat in today's world, supporting all the terrorists from Hamas [a Palestinian socio-political and militant Sunni movement] to Hezbollah [a Shia Islamist political and paramilitary organization] to some other terrorists that we don't know their names yet," and that "Iran destabilized the region by supporting all the illegal activities and activists such as Hamas." Ahmed Aboul Gheit, the Egyptian foreign minister, in a press conference in Anakara, ranted against Hezbollah's leader Hassan Nasrallah, saying that the Iranian-run terror organization had "practically declared war on Egypt."

Fighting Iranian Influence

So it is not totally surprising that Egyptian intelligence chief Omar Suleiman reportedly told the Israelis that Egypt wouldn't oppose a quick strike designed to bring down Hamas, or that Palestinian Authority chief Abu Mazen blames Hamas, which is largely an Iranian proxy [substitute], for the fighting. Israeli opposition leader Binyamin Netanyahu called for "toppling the Hamas rule over the [Gaza] Strip and uprooting the Iranian base there," which is probably what most Arab leaders want, even as they prepare to denounce Israel at the upcoming Wednesday [December 31, 2008] meeting of the Arab League (the best portrayal of which can be seen in David Lean's magisterial film *Lawrence of Arabia*). It is also what the United States should want, instead of pursuing the mirage of a Middle Eastern peace that cannot possibly be accomplished so long as the mullahs [religious leaders] rule in Tehran. They will continue their 30-year proxy war against the infidels until they either win or lose, and Israel will always be one of their prime targets. [Traveler and blogger] David Horvitz implores us to remember the Iranian connection, and he rightly says that at least some countries might support an action that defeats a major Iranian initiative.

The less serious component of the war has to do with domestic Israeli politics. The current crowd . . . is facing an election in a couple of months and has no chance of being returned to office if mortars, missiles, and rockets continue to fly into Israeli towns and cities from the Gaza Strip. Ergo, the air attack. There are those who believe that the Israeli Army will soon move into Gaza as well. As the 2006 war against the

Iranians' Hezbollah demonstrated, you can't destroy a terrorist organization from the air alone, and Olmert/Livni/Barak [Israeli political leaders] lost a great deal of public support when they failed to eliminate Hezbollah. They certainly don't want a repeat of that political debacle.

There cannot be peace in the Middle East so long as the mullahs wage war and think they're winning.

An Invasion Is Unlikely

I would be surprised if the army does invade. These Israeli leaders have been minimalists, and an invasion of Gaza would require both a kind of nerve they have not shown before and the courage to challenge the global community of negotiators (a/k/a appeasers) and thereby risk losing their seat at the big dining-room tables of world capitals. Still, life is full of surprises, and if the air war fails to stop the missile, mortar, and rocket attacks from Gaza (and as of Monday [December 29, 2008] evening, Washington time, they were still flying and still killing Israeli civilians), Olmert/Livni/Barak may feel compelled to take further risks.

Meanwhile, what of the terrorists? Some may be surprised that most of the pictures Hamas has provided to the international media have shown dead fighters, officials, and police, rather than civilians. True, very few civilians have been killed, but that has never stopped Hamas and its ilk from providing photographic "evidence" that later turned out to be phony. The presentation of their own dead is of a piece with their ideology; it is a glorification of martyrdom, part of a broader call to arms, a hymn to the cult of death that inspires the jihad [Holy War]. And the high priest of that cult is Iranian President Mahmoud Ahmadinejad, who has often spoken of martyrdom as the highest calling (for others, mind you, certainly not for himself). Please do not tell me that this cannot be, since the Iranians are Shiites and Hamas is Sunni; radical Shiites and Palestinian terrorists have been in cahoots for at least 37 years. Hamas gets weapons, training, intelligence, and money from the mullahs in return for doing their bidding. It's all about Iran, you see.

And please don't tell me that this only proves the urgency of diplomacy. It proves the opposite. There cannot be peace in the Middle East so long as the mullahs wage war and think they're winning. All those martyrs are viewed as signs of progress in Tehran.

The Threat of an Atomic Bomb

The Israelis know all this, just as they know that the mullahs are building an atomic bomb destined for Israeli territory. But Israel is a small country, despite the paranoid visions of some Western ideologues who think the Israelis run the world through espionage and lobbying. Iran is more than ten times the size of Israel, and even the most feisty Israeli shrinks from the thought of an open war with Tehran. So they are left to contend with the tentacles of the terrorist hydra [a mythological, multiheaded monster], while the main body remains untouched. They may chop off a piece of Hamas or Hezbollah, but it will regenerate and grab them again.

Not that the defeat of Iranian proxies is a small matter. The United States thrashed their proxy, al-Qaeda in Iraq, and in so doing rounded up a considerable number of Iranian military and intelligence officers who were playing their usual role of consiglieri [adviser] to the jihadis. Some senior Iranians have defected to the West, and the mullahs have still not managed to break the will of the pro-democracy dissidents in their own country, despite a record pace of killing that puts Iran in the running for the world's leading executioner (they are currently running second only to China, whose population is about 20 times Iran's).

25

This bespeaks a profound insecurity. It is the behavior of a regime that knows its people despise it, and, like all such tyrannies, it combines domestic terror with foreign adventure in order to preserve its position. For extras, the Iranian zealots at the top of the oppressive pyramid embrace an apocalyptic vision according to which the Last Days are upon us and the hoped-for coming of the Twelfth Imam [whose arrival signals the world's end for some Muslims] will be best catalyzed by global bloodshed and chaos.

Thus, the best Israel can hope to accomplish is to buy time, praying that somehow or other the Iranian regime will fall before the mullahs launch their promised genocidal attack, or that the Israelis will find a way to destroy the atomic weapon before it is used against them, or that the West will, at the eleventh hour, recognize that Iran is a global threat and find a way to thwart it.

It's a hell of a position to be in, and discussions of tactics and methods in Gaza address only a small part of the problem. The real problem isn't even being discussed.

4

Diplomacy Is Crucial to Defuse the Iran Problem

Suzanne Maloney and Ray Takeyh

Suzanne Maloney is a Senior Fellow of Foreign Policy at the Saban Center for Middle East Policy. Ray Takeyh is a Senior Fellow at the Council on Foreign Relations.

Iran's president Mahmoud Ahmadinejad's inflammatory comments have been used to portray Iran as a threat to global security. Yet while its support of terrorism and its anti-Israel stance remain dangerous, the U.S. needs to engage in serious diplomacy instead of weighing military options. It should work with Iran's neighbors to thwart the country's nuclear ambitions, and offer help and security to all those who will aid efforts to contain the situation. While a military option cannot be ruled out, it is time to have a dialogue with Iran.

Iran's president, Mahmoud Ahmadinejad, must sometimes strike Washington as the gift that keeps on giving. His odious [hateful] statements on the Holocaust and Israel, his nuclear defiance and his disastrous domestic policies have produced outrage at home and around the world. Yet even his best efforts haven't been enough to help the Bush administration build an international consensus around its floundering diplomatic approach.

The stalemate in talks and Washington's escalating allegations of Iranian malfeasance [misconduct] in Iraq have fueled speculation that the United States might strike Iran before George W. Bush leaves office. No matter what the administration does for its final act, however, it's still likely to bequeath the problem to its successor. Barring the unexpected, the next U.S. president will confront an array of threats similar to today's. Fortunately, he or she will have plenty of options that Bush has discarded, overlooked or just plain ignored.

Washington must figure out how to regulate Iran's power and diminish its unsavory practices.

Iran Is a Threat

Iran will, to be sure, remain a knotty problem. Tehran's quest for weapons of mass destruction, its support for terrorism, its antagonism toward Israel and the peace process, and its repression of domestic rights and freedoms have been consistent elements of the clerical [religious] regime's policy for most of its 28-year history. Bush's successor will face an Iran whose strategic position has been immeasurably strengthened by the elimination of powerful adversaries in Iraq and Afghanistan, and by the fact that the U.S. military remains bogged down in both places. The next American president will face an Iranian regime that is flush with oil money, essentially impervious to financial pressures and indifferent to U.S. threats. Perhaps most dangerous, he or she will have to grapple with a greatly accelerated Iranian nuclear program.

That said, the next president will inherit one big advantage. Simply not being George W. Bush—who even Iran's relatively pragmatic former president Ali Akbar Hashemi Rafsanjani has dismissed as a "dinosaur with a sparrow's brain"—will enormously improve the next president's prospects for dialogue.

The challenge will be how to take advantage of this opening. Washington must figure out how to regulate Iran's power and diminish its unsavory practices. Although the model of Chinese-American rapprochement is often invoked, a more suitable example is the détente [reduction in the tension between nations] pursued between the United States and the U.S.S.R. during the 1970s, when the two powers came together not because of any mutual fears (as was the case with the U.S.-Chinese opening) but out of a desire to stabilize their increasingly dangerous competition. Of course, Iran today is not the Soviet Union of that era. But Henry Kissinger's approach—creating mutually reinforcing commercial and diplomatic incentives to persuade adversaries to avoid conflict and conform to international norms—is just as relevant now as it was then.

Should Tehran cross successive nuclear thresholds in defiance of its international obligations and the United Nations' mandates, its neighbors are likely to become more willing to participate in a robust containment policy.

Tough Diplomacy Could Be Key

In the case of Iran, applying this means beginning a comprehensive dialogue that puts all the major issues on the table. Solutions will involve a series of trade-offs. If it wants to maintain some kind of civilian nuclear-power program, Iran should be told that it must agree to an unprecedented, intrusive verification scheme involving permanent inspectors and 24-hour monitoring of its facilities. In exchange for U.S. recognition of Iran's role in Iraq, Tehran should be expected to rein in the recalcitrant [stubborn] Shiite militias there and help set up a government that includes all of Iraq's factions. In exchange for Washington's acceptance of the legitimacy of Iran's clerical regime and the resumption of economic ties, Iran will have to stop meddling in the Israeli-Palestinian conflict. The Islamic Republic [of Iran] does not have to recognize Israel or dissolve Hizbullah [a Shia Islamist political and paramilitary organization based in Lebanon]. But it should abandon its public attacks on the Jewish state and press its Lebanese protégé to become a regular political party.

If none of the above works, of course, the next administration must be ready with a plan B. Today, the only fail-safe option Bush seems to favor is a military strike on Iran's atomic facilities. But this wouldn't offer a permanent solution to the Iranian nuclear problem or help stabilize Iraq or the Gulf (in fact, it would do just the opposite). A new backup plan is therefore needed, one that would help contain an empowered Iran and negate the impact of its nuclear weapons. Fortunately, crafting one will become easier as the danger from Iran intensifies. Should Tehran cross successive nuclear thresholds in defiance of its international obligations and the United Nations' mandates, its neighbors are likely to become more willing to participate in a robust containment policy. Europe and Japan, meanwhile—and even Russia and China—may finally agree to impose real sanctions.

America Must Use All Options

If talks fail, the United States should also issue a set of public warnings—much clearer and less blustery than those offered by the Bush administration. The Islamic Republic will have to be told that any first use of its bombs would constitute a direct threat against the United States. In a similar vein, any transfer of Iran's nuclear material would be viewed as a danger to the United States itself—and Washington would respond accordingly. The next president should also quietly offer Iran's neighbors informal security guarantees to ease their nerves and make them less inclined to acquiesce to Iranian blackmail. Such a concerted strategy would help Washington deny Iran any diplomatic leverage while building a formidable wall around it.

Even then, diplomacy will remain crucial. Should Iran at any point signal that it's ready to come in from the cold and dismantle its nukes, the United States should be prepared to engage it. None of this will be easy. But improving on the Bush administration's woefully ineffective approach won't prove that difficult, either.

5

Sanctions and Diplomacy Are the Answers to Iran's Nuclear Threat

Andrew Grotto

Andrew Grotto is a senior national security analyst at the Center for American Progress Action Fund in Washington, D.C. He is the author of Contain and Engage: A New Strategy for Resolving the Nuclear Crisis with Iran.

So far, efforts to curtail Iran's nuclear program have failed. Although Iran doesn't seem willing to back off, its neighbors have a vested interest in reducing the threat Iran poses to peace in the Middle East and beyond. With multi-lateral support, Washington should engage in diplomacy to learn more about Iran's ambitions and intentions, and to make informed decisions about the future course of its policies.

Over the weekend, Iran rebuffed the latest effort by world powers to jumpstart negotiations over its controversial nuclear programme. At a meeting in Geneva last month, they had proposed a "freeze-for-freeze" under which Iran would suspend efforts to install more centrifuges, the so-called P5+1 would halt efforts to enact new international sanctions and the two sides would spend six weeks negotiating over whether to have formal negotiations over Iran's programme.

The P5+1—China, France, Germany, Russia, the United Kingdom and the United States—gave Iran two weeks to respond. That deadline tolled Saturday, when Iran's president Mahmoud Ahmadinejad pledged that "the Iranian nation will not give up a single iota of its nuclear rights."

So the freeze-for-freeze gambit failed. What's next for the P5+1?

Iran is clearly not in a negotiating frame of mind, at least on the nuclear issue. And why would it be? The game is rigged in its favour. Oil prices are at record levels, which furnish ample resources to ride out limited UN sanctions, and Tehran's influence over the course of events in Afghanistan and Iraq give it direct leverage over the security interests of the US and its allies.

What the P5+1—and the Bush administration in particular—need to do is change the rules of the game to magnify the pressures on Iran. There are four key moves they should make.

Iran is clearly not in a negotiating frame of mind, at least on the nuclear issue.

First, the P5+1 should immediately seek a fourth sanctions resolution targeting Iran's senior leadership. Sanctioning Iran where it would hurt most—its petroleum sector—is improbable because few countries seem willing to bear the costs it would exact on the global economy. So sanctions alone are unlikely to force Iran's leaders to swallow the bitter pill of compromise on the nuclear issue. But Iran's leaders must incur some cost for their defiance, and a fourth resolution would remind them—as well as the rest of the world—that the UN security council is united behind the aim of ending Iran's enrichment programme.

Second, the Bush administration should wholeheartedly embrace senator Barack Obama's proposal—all but endorsed last month by Iraq's Prime Minister Nouri al-Maliki—for a responsible, phased redeployment of US forces from Iraq by the end of 2010. In addition to forcing Iraqi leaders to take direct responsibility for their country and relieving a terrible burden on America's military personnel and fiscal health, this proposal would eliminate a key source of leverage for Iran and could force it to use its influence in Iraq more constructively.

Third, the Bush administration should do whatever it can to knock Syria from Iran's orbit, including offers of incentives if necessary. This will be difficult, but well worth the effort. Syria is Iran's only real ally in the region. It is an important channel for Iran to funnel money and influence to groups like Hizbullah in Lebanon.

In negotiations over the nuclear programme, the Iranians have already indicated they seek a broader dialogue.

But the partnership has left Syria increasingly isolated in the region, and there are signs that it may be ready to cut a deal with the west to break out of its isolation. It has already engaged Israel in Turkish-mediated discussions aimed at securing a comprehensive peace between the two longtime adversaries. And its president, Bashir Assad, travelled to Tehran over the weekend at the request of France to try and persuade the Iranians to be more cooperative on the nuclear issue.

Finally, the Bush administration should be open to direct bilateral talks with the Iranians on any issue. In negotiations over the nuclear programme, the Iranians have already indicated they seek a broader dialogue. Washington should grant it. In general, talking with Iran will produce better information about its intentions and vulnerabilities, yield more policy options and ultimately lead to better, more informed US policy. These discussions should be separate from P5+1 negotiations so as to not distract attention from the 800-lb gorilla—the nuclear programme—that Iran would just as soon not talk about. At the beginning this could entail establishing a US interests section in Tehran—which the Bush administration recently floated—and freeing up diplomats there and around the world to seek interactions with their Iranian counterparts, a practice that is currently prohibited.

All this, of course, is a tall order for any presidency in its waning months, particularly one as set in its ways as the Bush administration. And none of these issues are likely to be resolved anyway before its term is up in January 2009. But President Bush could do a great service to both international security and his successor by getting the ball rolling now.

6

The Outcome of More Diplomatic Talks with Iran Is Uncertain

Jan De Pauw

Jan De Pauw is a lecturer in cultural history and media at Erasmus Hogeschool, Brussels.

While claims from the Bush administration about the danger of Iran's nuclear program seem, in light of new evidence, overstated, America will still face a difficult path dealing with Iran. The relationship of the two countries has been marred by insincerity, support for undemocratic regimes, covert military actions, and sabotage. A more pragmatic United States approach, that steps away from talks of military strikes; a more coherent security council; and active mediation by a strong European Alliance might be three key ingredients to unlock the Iran problem.

The status and intentions of Iran's nuclear-energy plans are again at the top of the international agenda, and in a dramatic and unexpected way. The publication of the latest United States national-intelligence estimate (NIE) on 3 December 2007—in the declassified digest released to the public—contained the striking assessment that Iran halted its nuclear-weapons programme in 2003 "in response to international pressure"; a judgment, moreover, backed with "high confidence".

Jan De Pauw, "Iran, the United States and Europe: The Nuclear Complex," *Open Democracy*, May 12, 2007. This article was originally published in the independent online magazine *www.opendemocracy.net*.

A Political Challenge

The report, which gathers material from the US's sixteen leading intelligence agencies, does admit: "We do not know whether [Iran] currently intends to develop nuclear weapons". But the tenor of the report is—as has been instantly understood around the world—to challenge the narrative of an Iranian nuclear danger that the George W. Bush administration and its supporters has assiduously been building, and to make more difficult the argument for armed confrontation with Iran as a way of resolving the perceived problem.

Iran's own reaction has, predictably, been both satisfied and combative: the president, Mahmoud Ahmadinejad, called the report's conclusions "a declaration of the Iranian people's victory against the great powers", while Tehran has also called on the US to abandon its plans to seek a new tranche [installment] of sanctions on Iran in the United Nations [UN] Security Council. Meanwhile, the head of the International Atomic Energy Agency (IAEA), Mohamed ElBaradei, has acknowledged that the verdict "opens a window of opportunity for Iran now because Iran obviously has been somewhat vindicated in saying they have not been working on a weapons programme at least for the last few years".

This single report has evidently changed the atmospherics in which the debate has for long been conducted, even if its key conclusion over Iran is hardly accepted by all interested parties (not least Israel). But when the dust settles, how much will have changed? Will the world know any more about Iran's "real" nuclear plans or intentions than before? To answer these questions, it is helpful to review the recent history of this contentious international issue, and in particular the attempts of leading interlocutors [participants]—the European Union [EU] as well as the IAEA and the United States—to deal with Iran.

The Springtime of Diplomacy

The weeks before the NIE report was released did not promise much in the way of diplomatic progress. Iran's new nuclear negotiator Saeed Jalili had at stroke annulled [undone] much of the work of his predecessor Ali Larijani, disappointed Europe's foreign-policy chief Javier Solana, deepened suspicions over Iran's hardline agenda and kindled the idea of a third round of UN sanctions. In the West, there was outward support from Britain and France for the US's strong line at the Security Council, against equally routine reluctance from China and Russia. But at a meeting in Paris on 1 December 2007 of the European Union's troika [a team of three] on Iran—Britain, France and Germany, the "EU/E3" (or "EU3")—Germany this time seemed, if only faintly, to hesitate. The Iran nuclear issue seems to have an uncanny capacity to create tensions between supposed partners.

Indeed, Iran has been the strongest test-case of the European Union's nuclear non-proliferation strategy since its inauguration in June 2003. The strategy called for a broad approach to proliferation threats, including preventative measures (both political and diplomatic) to be implemented through relevant international organisations, as well as coercive measures under Chapter VII of the UN charter and international law. The strategy is part of what has been called a policy of "effective multilateralism".

Will the world know any more about Iran's "real" nuclear plans or intentions than before?

The first rumours about Iran's nuclear military ambitions emerged in 2002. By June 2003, the International Atomic Energy Agency, after inspections at Natanz and Arak, confirmed Iran's fissile activities and recommended that Iran sign the additional protocol to the 1970 nuclear non-proliferation treaty (to which the country was and is a signatory). By October

2003—lightning-speed in diplomatic terms—the EU signed an agreement with Tehran through the joint efforts of Britain, France and Germany.

Indeed, Iran has been the strongest test-case of the European Union's nuclear non-proliferation strategy since its inauguration in June 2003.

A Diplomatic Achievement

In this document—what came to be known as the Tehran agreement—Iran consented to suspending all enrichment activities and promised to sign the additional protocol; the *quid pro quo* [something given or received for something else] for Tehran was further negotiations. This was considered a major diplomatic achievement for Europe: the premiere of an EU speaking with one voice and wielding "soft power" to good effect. The agreement effectively positioned the EU/E3 between the two main contenders—Iran and the United States—as well as strengthened the role of the IAEA.

By spring 2004, however, both the US and the IAEA independently denounced Iran's erratic behaviour with regard to the Tehran agreement. In September [2004], Iran itself followed up its initial threats by effectively and publicly resuming its uranium-conversion activities. It is not improbable that pressure over the forthcoming (June 2005) general elections in Iran hardened then-president Mohammad Khatami's stance on his country's nuclear rights. Meanwhile, the US, under the spell of a highly divisive presidential election campaign, was becoming increasingly impatient about Iran's behaviour.

When the US demanded that Iran be referred to the Security Council, the EU/E3 rose to the challenge: again, it secured a deal with Iran in November 2004 that promised broader negotiations, economic benefits and technological assistance for

Iran's civilian nuclear programme. But the pattern was repeated: by May 2005, this deal—the Paris agreement—was coming undone.

Until this point, Europe's interaction with Iran closely resembled its 1990s policy of "critical dialogue" with Iran: an inclusive and comprehensive strategy of relationship-building and economic engagement that might give Europe leverage over contentious issues such as human rights, freedom, torture, terrorism and weapons of mass destruction. But in June 2005, the neo-conservative Mahmoud Ahmadinejad won the presidential election and inherited office from the more moderate but disappointing Khatami. The surprise victory of the relatively unknown ex-mayor of Tehran was followed by a swift change of tone. Iran's interaction both with the EU/E3, and with the IAEA and the US, became more confrontational.

The Sanctions Spiral

The EU/E3 offered Ahmadinejad a framework for a long-term agreement that—amongst other things—proposed specific security guarantees, areas of cooperation and long-term support for Iran's civil nuclear programme. The offer was promptly rejected and the talks between Iran and the EU broke down. Europe's lack of success, however, was compensated to some degree by its ability to convince Russia and China to refrain from using their veto to block an IAEA resolution on Iran's non-compliance with the IAEA safeguards agreement. But by this time, another threat was looming: multilateral sanctions, this time endorsed by the UN Security Council.

By January 2006, Iran had again resumed enrichment, and by February the country was effectively referred to the UN Security Council. By 29 March, Iran was given another deadline one month hence; this it ignored. A phase of clever manoeuvring all around briefly raised hopes of direct talks between Iran and the US in a multilateral setting; in large part, that too was an EU/E3 accomplishment, as was the extensive package of incentives put together by the EU/E3, China, Russia and the US offered to Iran in June 2006 by Europe's foreign-policy supremo, Javier Solana.

The July–August 2006 war in Lebanon and the contested victory of the Iran-backed Hizbollah [a Shia Islamist political and paramilitary organization based in Lebanon] movement left the regime in Tehran feeling sufficiently bolstered to dismiss Solana's proposals. In the feverish months of August–September 2006, the EU/E3 were granted the privilege of keeping up the appearance of a constructive dialogue. By October [2006], even Solana acknowledged that "four months of intensive talks have brought no agreement on suspension" and that one "can't go on talking forever". The EU/E3 then submitted a draft resolution to the UN to curtail Iran by means of sanctions. After prolonged debate, and Russian and Chinese amendments, Resolution 1737 was unanimously adopted by the UN Security Council on 23 December 2006.

A Twist in the Tale

The twin electoral victories of Democrats in the United States (in the mid-term elections of November 2006) and reformers in Iran (in the local elections of December 2006) did not soften positions on either side. Indeed, by March 2007, a second round of UN sanctions was unanimously accepted, the rhetoric of war resounded ever louder, and the middle ground occupied by the EU/E3 tilted toward stronger (and by late 2007, possibly even unilateral) sanctions.

In this sense, there has been a definite shift of approach in Europe's policy towards Iran. The stance of the "critical dialogue" period seems to have been exchanged for the second leg of its non-proliferation strategy: namely the implementation of coercive measures in the context of Chapter VII of the UN charter. Europe may have been consistent in relation to its own policy recommendations of diplomacy first, coercion later (or last), but with regard to another of its strategy's basic principles—the implementation and universalisation of existing disarmament and non-proliferation norms—it has been wholly unsuccessful. Europe's position as a putative mediator between the US and Iran has suffered as a result.

The twin electoral victories of Democrats in the United States . . . and reformers in Iran . . . did not soften positions on either side.

As a result, Europe's lack of leverage over American behaviour in the international arena has carried a cost, in three respects.

First, American support for Europe's diplomatic track has always been half-hearted; the George W. Bush administration has never really taken unilateral military action towards Iran off the shelf (nor is this out of the question even after the NIE report of 3 December 2007). Throughout, Europe has never been able to secure a full diplomatic engagement from the US.

Second, the US's nuclear deal with India—an established nuclear-weapons state—was a signal to Iran that there really was nothing to be gained from compliance with the international community's demands.

Third, Europe's continued hesitation about America's proposed deployment of a missile-defence system in east-central Europe both soured relations with Russia (an important partner regarding UN Security Council decisions on Iran) and suggested that Europe in fact accepts the "truth" and the threat of a nuclear-armed Iran. The EU/E3 thus gradually revealed itself as less a detached mediator and more America's coalition partner finally let out of the closet.

Maybe Diplomacy Has Not Failed

The margins for diplomacy have been narrowing since at least June 2005, and rumours and rhetoric of armed confrontation increasing. Throughout 2007, the path to war has seemed ever less avoidable. It is in this context that the US's latest national-intelligence estimate seems to many observers to offer almost miraculous deliverance.

Will it be so? The finding that, after all, Iran had already abandoned the military aspect of its nuclear programme in 2003, following increased diplomatic pressure, suggests that the history of the last five years—whose outlines are traced in this article—may have to be rewritten. The new NIE assessment certainly undermines the official line of imminent military threat, and potentially reconnects with the diplomatic approach favoured by most of the international community and the IAEA.

The margins for diplomacy have been narrowing since at least June 2005, and rumours and rhetoric of armed confrontation increasing.

Yet, the implication of the foregoing analysis is that diplomatic advances or signs of progress in the long-running dispute between Iran and the West—especially the United States—are so often followed by severe setbacks. The best-case result may be that the intelligence assessment may reduce America's taste for war, fortify the next American president's conviction to stay on the diplomatic track and re-establish Europe's locomotive role in designing a deal with Iran that—this time—will last. The worst-case result may be that the objective alliance between Mahmoud Ahmadinejad, Saeed Jalili and the Iranian neo-conservatives with their United States counterparts proves too strong and addictive to break. In either case, the tortuous diplomatic story of Iran, the United States, [and] Europe over Iran's nuclear plans has a long way to go.

7

Delaying a Decisive Response to an Iranian Threat Might Prove Fatal

John Bolton

John Bolton is a senior fellow at the American Enterprise Institute for Public Policy Research. Before joining AEI, he served as undersecretary of state for arms control and international security and as U.S. permanent representative to the United Nations.

The history of intelligence gathering in Iran shows that, again and again, America has based its policies involving Iran on misinformation. The situation in Iran is a precarious one because there is no one certainty regarding how far along the regime has come in building a full-fledged nuclear program. Although diplomacy has its place, negotiations with Iran have failed consistently. Neither America nor Europe has succeeded in gaining concessions from Tehran. The military option is unattractive, but with Iran threatening Israel, the Israeli government might decide to strike strategic targets and attempt to destroy Iran's nuclear facilities. A nuclear-armed Iran is a prospect too dangerous to be ignored.

The topic that we're trying to address [when this work was delivered on October 22, 2008] is the subject of Iran and looking ahead to the next Administration, so I want to try and focus on the issues that the next Administration is going to face. But I think that necessarily involves looking back a

Honorable John Bolton, "Iran and the Next Administration: Policy Challenges," *Heritage Lecture # 1104*, January 14, 2009. Copyright © 2009 The Heritage Foundation. Reproduced by permission.

little bit at some of what's happened over the past several years and how we got to that point and to identify some of the things that I think the next President, whoever it turns out to be, has to address, and in a very urgent manner, because the threat posed by Iran's effort to acquire deliverable nuclear weapons capability is an urgent threat for which there's not much room for error.

Iran's effort to acquire mastery over the entire nuclear fuel cycle is simply consistent with no other alternative explanation . . . than that they seek nuclear weapons.

The first broad area is the question of American intelligence about what Iran is doing: what we know, what we don't know, how we analyze what we know. And this is a subject of considerable importance since many of our friends, and particularly many of our adversaries, invariably say whenever we talk about Iran or North Korea or other would-be proliferators, "Well, how can you be so sure? After all, look how wrong you were on Iraq." . . .

Certainly it is a fair point for critics of the United States or for policymakers in the United States itself to have a skepticism about what we think we know about any subject, not just proliferation. It also is fair, as the Bush Administration leaves office and some of the particular controversies that surrounded the subject of intelligence fade a little bit, that we have a discussion about American intelligence capabilities: where they're strong and where they're not, where they have failed us in recent years and where they can be improved.

I think that's pertinent to Iran for a number of reasons, not the least of which is that you can be very, very worried about Iran's nuclear weapons program without having access to intelligence. I think a fair reading of the many reports over the last five or six years from the International Atomic Energy Agency, the huge amount of information about Iran's effort to acquire mastery over the entire nuclear fuel cycle is simply consistent with no other alternative explanation for Iran's behavior than that they seek nuclear weapons.

Intelligence Analysis

But I think it's also important to look at not simply the information that's available, but for what follows that in the form of what we call "intelligence analysis." Just in the past couple of years, we've seen in the United States some of the real problems associated with defective analysis within the intelligence community, defective structures within the intelligence community, and defective policy conclusions that flow from all of that.

The fact is that there's always a risk of the politicization of intelligence.

I think this goes to some very basic questions that we should have more discussion of in public in the next Administration. If you look at the comments that many Members of Congress have made over the past several years—for example, criticizing the Bush Administration for cherry-picking intelligence about Iraq, or some of the more extreme criticisms, such as making up intelligence about Iraq and inferentially cherry-picking or making up intelligence about any other subject, including Iran's program—I think you can see some of the reasons for concern.

Intelligence and Policymaking

You can also see it in the hypocritical and inconsistent approaches many people take to intelligence versus policymaking. On the one hand, you have people who say absolutely there should be a wall of separation between intelligence and policymaking when it suits their purposes to say it, but who take a very different attitude when intelligence analysis leaks out of the intelligence community and finds itself being published in the major media, as if intelligence analysis—and particularly National Intelligence Estimates—is like the reports that think tanks issue from time to time. We get everybody together in the intelligence community, they review the most sensitive information that we have, and then we publish it in the *New York Times* because it's a contribution to the national debate.

The fact is that there's always a risk of the politicization of intelligence. There's a risk that policymakers will politicize intelligence, and there's a risk that intelligence analysts will politicize intelligence because it suits their analytical preferences to do so.

I think there's also a misconception about what basic intelligence is. Again, to listen to some Members of Congress, you'd think there's all this information. There's what's reported in the newspapers; there's what's reported in diplomatic cables back from posts around the world; there's speculation; there's what people in the private sector learn; and then there's intelligence, which is carried out on a silver platter as if this is the answer to everything, and if you disagree with a piece of intelligence, somehow you're beyond the pale. Or, more to the point, if you disagree with intelligence analysis that happens to suit a particular Senator or House Member's predilection, you're beyond the pale.

The Perfect Storm

I think that we've seen perhaps the perfect storm of intelligence failure concerning Iran over the years, over and over again: lacking information because we don't have adequate sources inside Iran, reliance on foreign intelligence services, and re-analysis of existing data over and over again because of political imperatives within the intelligence community.

I can't tell you how many times, during my service in government in the [George W.] Bush 43 Administration, people would troop down from one or another intelligence agency to say, "Okay, we've revised our estimate on when Iran will actually have everything it needs for a nuclear weapon." Sometimes they'd come down and say, "It's longer than the last time that we talked to you." Sometimes they'd come down and say, "It's shorter than the last time we talked to you."

In almost every case, I'd say to them, "Well, I follow this very closely. What new facts have emerged that lead you to this new conclusion?" And all too frequently, the answer was, "Nothing really that you haven't seen, but we've just been thinking about it again, and we've revised our conclusions accordingly."

I don't think there's any doubt that the National Intelligence Estimate that concluded that Iran had suspended its nuclear weapons program in the fall of 2003 was written reflecting the political biases of its authors. I think that the way it was written, to have a very narrow definition of what amounts to a nuclear weapons program, reflects that. When congressional staff said, "Why did you use that definition of a nuclear weapons program, which was principally weaponization, design, and fabrication?" their response was, "That's the definition the Iranians use." *There's* a compelling reason to accept it!

The idea that you can force everything into broad consensus, and the fact that so much time and effort is spent on this as a priority, is very misguided.

A Weak White House

I think the consequence of publication of the major conclusions of that National Intelligence Estimate, even though done with the acquiescence of the White House, reflects the overt politicization of the intelligence community. It was written in a way that was designed to be leaked if a weakened White

House hadn't given its acquiescence, and the fact that the White House was weak and succumbed to it is no justification for the way that report was put together.

In fact, I would go further, and I think this is an issue for the next Administration across the board in the intelligence community: I'm not at all sure that we shouldn't cease the publication of National Intelligence Estimates. I'm not at all sure that the drive for consensus of evaluation within the intelligence community is a sensible way to proceed. Personally, I believe in intellectual competition, and if intelligence agencies have data and have analysis that's persuasive, they ought to be willing to put it out within the community of policymakers—not in the *New York Times* and other publications, but in a classified setting—and let policymakers and other intelligence analysts debate it.

The idea that you can force everything into broad consensus, and the fact that so much time and effort is spent on this as a priority, is very misguided. That's something that obviously goes well beyond Iran, but we're going to see it in particular in Iran because of the critical element in intelligence that most policymakers look at, which is when will Iran have what it takes to have a deliverable nuclear weapon? That's probably the single most important question and one that I don't think we've gotten good answers to over the years.

Negotiation is not a policy. Negotiation is a technique.

Diplomacy and Negotiation

The reason that is such an important question relates to the second area I wanted to cover today, which is diplomacy and negotiation with Iran. Looking at intelligence estimates on timing—which are good-faith judgments by people who can disagree over exactly what point it is we really need to worry about in assessing Iran's domestic mastery over the entire nuclear fuel cycle and its weaponization and delivery capability—a lot of people say, "The estimates say we've got two years before Iran has a deliverable nuclear weapon. Two years is forever in the diplomatic world. We're not in any rush. We don't have to feel constrained. We've got plenty of time to continue to explore diplomatic options."

Personally, I do not believe in "just in time" nonproliferation, because if you can imagine that the intelligence estimate is wrong, then Iran or another would-be proliferator has the weapons capability before our estimates indicated, and the entire context of diplomacy—indeed, the entire international geopolitical context—has changed. I think that's especially true as we see a new Administration coming in, whether it's Senator John McCain or Senator Barack Obama [Obama, in fact, won], because they will hear over and over again, certainly from the State Department and from many, many commentators, "You've got to give diplomacy a try." Senator Obama himself has said he would sit down with the Iranians without precondition to discuss their nuclear program.

This is a statement about diplomacy that I think warrants considerable attention on several levels. First, negotiation is not a policy. Negotiation is a technique. It's like asking the question, "Do you want to eat with a fork or a spoon?" Well, what are you trying to eat? That's the real question. If you want to eat soup with a fork, it's a little bit of a problem. Whether you use a spoon or a fork or a butter knife or anything else is a matter of technique, and in saying we should have negotiation with Iran, very little has been said about the substance of the negotiation.

Process Trumps Substance

This is already advance warning of State Department thinking, which is obsessed with process and less obsessed with substance. But it goes beyond simply confusing procedures with substance. It goes to a more important point, which is ignoring history in the case of Iran.

We have had five years of negotiation between the EU3—Britain, France, and Germany—and Iran, and it has been understood from the get-go by the Europeans, by the Iranians, and by the State Department that, in effect, the Europeans were speaking for us. And they have made the point from the very first meeting. When the three foreign ministers from Europe—dubbed by Secretary [Colin] Powell at the time "the three tenors"—all went off to Tehran, the message they carried was you can have a different relationship not just with us, but with the United States if you will give up uranium enrichment.

That has been the position right on through, and if there was any doubt about where we stood on the Europeans as surrogate negotiators for us, that was certainly cleared up in 2006 when Secretary [of State Condoleezza] Rice conveyed publicly that we would sit down in public with the Iranians if only they would suspend uranium enrichment, as they had consistently refused to do. In fact, we've even gone beyond that and have sat down in public in Geneva with the Iranians, and they hadn't suspended uranium enrichment.

While we have watched the Europeans pretend not to negotiate for five years, the Iranians have gotten five years closer to nuclear weapons.

The idea that the Europeans for five years have actually not been negotiating with Iran, but have simply been informing Iran that if Iran would meet the precondition of giving up uranium enrichment, then they would begin negotiation, is a complete charade, but an important one. What it means is that the Europeans, although saying there was a precondition for real negotiation, in fact were negotiating their little hearts out with the Iranians, providing every carrot they could think of to induce Iran to give up uranium enrichment without ever succeeding in doing so.

Negotiations Have Failed

What this proves—and I think this is important—is that negotiation with Iran is hardly a new idea. Quite the opposite: It's an old idea—an old idea that has failed—and it demonstrates very graphically a point that is missed by those who say, "Why don't we just negotiate with the Iranians?" Negotiation is no different from any other human activity: It has costs as well as benefits. I don't mean monetary costs; I mean opportunity costs. The fact is that the Iranians have benefited enormously from five years of failed European negotiation. They have been given an asset that they couldn't buy for love or money: They've been given five years of time.

Almost invariably, time works on the side of the would-be proliferators: time that they need to overcome the complex science and technology, the difficulties that they face in building a nuclear program; time that allows them, as in the case of Iran, to perfect the technique of uranium conversion and to perfect the technique of uranium enrichment; as well as time to continue to disperse their nuclear facilities and increase their military defenses around those facilities.

While we have watched the Europeans pretend not to negotiate for five years, the Iranians have gotten five years closer to nuclear weapons, and they are at a point where, within some margin of error, they have mastered the science and technology. They don't have the weapon capability yet, but they will achieve it essentially at a time and a manner of their choosing, and then the calculus will be very different.

Talks Won't Be Successful

So the idea that negotiation can go on forever or that it is an activity that doesn't include costs for the parties to the negotiation is an extraordinary fallacy, but one that too often permeates our views on what negotiation can do. In the case of Iran, I don't think there's any chance that Iran is going to be talked out of its nuclear weapons. There's no price that we can pay that will induce Iran to give up those nuclear weapons, and I think that was clear quite some time ago.

Now, while this chitchatting has been going on, we've been trying sanctions that the Russians have successfully neutered on every occasion we've tried them in the Security Council, to the point where just within the last month we made the suggestion for a fourth sanctions resolution. The Russians flatly rejected it, so instead, because, as I like to say, we never fail in New York—that's what all ambassadors in New York say— they passed a fourth resolution on sanctions that said essentially, "You know those last three resolutions? We really mean them."

I've heard from ambassadors directly from the Arab countries exactly how I feel about that resolution: It was an embarrassment. I don't know what the equivalent to popping champagne corks is in Tehran, but whatever the equivalent is, that's what they were doing when that fourth resolution was passed.

The Military Option

That brings me to the subject that I think should most concern the next President, and that's the use of military force against Iran's program. I once thought the Bush Administration might use military force, a targeted force against Iran's program, and I said that. I believed that because the President said repeatedly, "It is unacceptable for Iran to have nuclear weapons," and I used to say, "The President's a man of his word; if he says it's unacceptable, I think what he means by that is it's unacceptable."

Well, I guess it's unacceptable rhetorically, but it's not going to be unacceptable in operational terms.

I don't think this [Bush] Administration will use force before it leaves office; I think that option has disappeared. But I think it is an option that is under very active consideration in Israel. I don't believe that they have reached a decision there; I think the condition of their government at this point prevents it until there's greater clarity within the Israeli body politic. I don't know when that will come; I don't know what the new government will look like; but I think the odds are that until the political situation in Israel is clarified, there won't be a clear decision, absent some information on the state of play inside Iran that might force a decision.

I don't think there's any doubt that Israel has the political will to use military force against Iran's program. We know from the bombing of the Osirak reactor outside of Baghdad in 1981 and we know from last September [2007], when Israel destroyed that North Korean reactor being built on the banks of the Euphrates River, that, confronted with the prospect of a nuclear neighbor, a nuclear enemy nearby, Israel won't hesitate to strike.

It is a deeply unattractive option to consider the use of military force against Iran's nuclear program—deeply unattractive. It's risky; it may not succeed fully; it may not succeed at all; there are undoubtedly consequences that Israel would face. But I think from the Israeli point of view, and I think from the American point of view, however deeply unattractive the use of military force is, it is far more unattractive to contemplate an Iran with deliverable nuclear weapons.

Israel May Use Military Force

So I think it's at least possible that the situation in Israel will clarify itself before the end of this Administration, and I think, certainly after our election [for U.S. president in 2008], a government in Israel could decide that it's going to need to use military force and might conclude that it would be better to do that prior to the end of the Bush Administration rather than waiting until afterward. It may be that they're not ready or that they haven't accomplished the planning and preparation they need to and that it would stretch out some time into the future. I've heard estimates that people would be willing to contemplate waiting perhaps until the summer of next year [2009] before there absolutely had to be a decision on Israel's part whether to use military force, but I don't think anybody should doubt this is a very live option.

How would Iran respond to that? They have threatened all manner of things: closing the Strait of Hormuz, cutting off oil exports. I don't think either of those is going to happen, because I think they do more damage to Iran than they do to the other powers in the region and to the United States. I think the more likely Iranian response is to have Hezbollah [a Shia Islamist political and paramilitary organization based in Lebanon] attack Israel—Hezbollah, reflecting the failure of Security Council Resolution 1701, probably resupplied and re-armed better than it was before the August 2006 adoption of Resolution 1701, with longer range, perhaps more accurate missiles, and with a real risk, therefore, of causing considerable casualties and damage inside Israel.

That's one of the factors—one of the very hard factors—Israel's decision-makers have to consider in contemplating military force. But again, I think, weighed against the prospect of what they see and what President George W. Bush once described as a nuclear holocaust, that military force is very much at the top of their minds and, therefore, the consequences of the use of military force, if it happens before January 20 [2009], or the prospect of it happening afterwards, are things that the next [U.S.] President needs to confront.

What all of this says to me is that the lesson that you have to draw on proliferation by states like Iran is that you can fiddle around for a long time before you see the real consequences, but if you fiddle just a little bit too long, those consequences are going to be dire indeed.

8

Hyping the Nuclear Threat from Iran Might Cause War in the Middle East

Gregory Levey

Gregory Levey is the author of the memoir Shut Up, I'm Talking: And Other Diplomacy Lessons I Learned in the Israeli Government. *He is on faculty at Ryerson University and blogs at Gregory Levey.com.*

Pro-Israel lobbyists are outspoken in their desire to strike Iran and force it to give up its nuclear program. They call for an end to diplomatic attempts and sanctions designed to thwart Iran's ambitions. The renewed hyperbole surrounding Iran might well prove enough to plunge America into a new war.

March 7, 2008 [R]ecently, I asked former Mossad officer Michael Ross what he thought of the latest U.S. National Intelligence Estimate released in December, which downplayed the threat posed by Iran's nuclear program. "That farce?" he replied, adding that many in Israeli intelligence were "furious about it—not just the conclusion of the estimate, but its timing as well." Some Iran hawks believe that the United Nations Security Council was poised at the time, with the United States leading the charge, to tighten the vice on the Iranian regime with tough new sanctions. But in the wake of the NIE's disclosure, there was a powerful shift in world opinion about Iran's alleged nuclear program, and the momentum was apparently lost.

Ross operated covertly inside Iran in the early 1990s, spying on the Iranian nuclear program for Israel, and worked closely with U.S. intelligence agencies, before retiring in 2001. His view of the NIE, which concluded that Iran had halted the weapons development aspect of its nuclear program in 2003, is similar to views held by hawkish intelligence officials and policy thinkers in the U.S. and Israel. On the Iranian issue in particular, there has long been a close relationship between the Israeli and U.S. governments, and the NIE's disclosure set off a flurry of activity in both countries. It had put hawks in an extraordinary position: If they wanted to keep up the pressure to go after Iran—using diplomacy and sanctions, or perhaps military force if deemed necessary—they would now have to discredit the highest-level intelligence report produced by the United States.

In Jerusalem, top Israeli leaders convened a meeting to decide how to deal with the problem. One result of the meeting was that when President Bush visited Israel in January, Israeli Defense Minister Ehud Barak was tasked with briefing him on Israeli intelligence on Iran, allegedly including some new information, in order to convince Bush to continue applying maximum pressure on Iran. "It's apparently true that in 2003 Iran stopped pursuing its military nuclear program for a time," Barak said then, "but in our opinion, since then it has apparently continued that program."

Meanwhile, in Washington, various interest groups with hard-line views on Iran and the Middle East have been working vigorously to refocus U.S. and world attention on Iran as an imminent threat. They include Evangelical Christians and conservative Jewish lobbyists—some with close ties to John McCain. The founder of one influential Evangelical group, who has made aggressive calls for attacking Iran, just endorsed McCain's run for the White House.

With McCain the presumptive Republican nominee, national security and instability in the Middle East are certain to return to the spotlight in the general campaign, as many McCain supporters believe those issues play to his strengths. The director of foreign policy for McCain's campaign said in an interview Wednesday that McCain remains "skeptical" of the latest NIE's findings, and outlined McCain's views on Iran in terms similar to those of some hawkish lobbyists working behind the scenes in Washington.

> *In Washington, various interest groups with hard-line views on Iran and the Middle east have been working vigorously to refocus U.S. and world attention on Iran as an imminent threat.*

On Monday, the U.N. Security Council voted to impose a new round of sanctions on Iran. The latest round will freeze the assets of some Iranian officials and companies connected to the nuclear program, as well as prohibit trade with Iran in certain supplies that have both civilian and military uses. Although hawks are somewhat heartened by this development, U.N. sanctions have effected little change in Tehran in the past, and for many of them the latest round is not enough.

David Brog, executive director of Christians United for Israel, has referred to the latest NIE as the "National Incompetence Estimate," and told me that CUFI is engaged in serious efforts to counter the reduced sense of urgency about Iran that it spawned. Although he hadn't yet had a chance to fully analyze the latest sanctions, he said his sense was that they were again relatively "soft," because that would've been "the only way to get consensus" at the U.N. Security Council. He said that his organization is pushing for all measures against Iran short of war—but also repeatedly stressed, "No one should take the military option off the table. It would be ill-advised diplomacy to assure Iran or any foe that there will never be military consequences to their actions."

Brog's group was founded by John Hagee, who serves as its national chairman. A fiery Evangelical Zionist who has openly called for a preemptive strike on Iran, Hagee endorsed John McCain's presidential run on Feb. 27.

At its annual conference in Washington last year, CUFI armed its attendees with talking points on Iran and sent them off to see their Congress members and senators, a strategy similar to that of the American Israel Public Affairs Committee, the powerful lobbying group. It is likely that both organizations will do the same thing at their annual conferences this summer, which will come at a time analysts believe could be fraught with danger in the Middle East because of Israel's escalating conflict with Hamas in Gaza, and continuing tensions between Israel and the Iranian-allied Hezbollah. Brog told me that he hopes the presidential nominees of both political parties will attend this year's CUFI conference in Washington.

Speaking at last year's conference, McCain told the crowd that the only thing worse than a military confrontation with Iran was a "nuclear armed Iran," and that the "regime must understand that it cannot win a showdown with the world." Since the NIE's release, McCain has been in the ranks of those dismissive of it. His campaign's director of foreign policy, Randy Scheunemann, told me Wednesday that "a careful reading of the NIE indicates that it is misleading." Scheunemann also said that McCain has been critical of the intelligence community for trying to "make policy" with the NIE. "There can be no doubt that the NIE harmed our efforts to achieve a greater diplomatic consensus" to crack down on Iran, he said.

It would be ill-advised diplomacy to assure Iran or any foe that there will never be military consequences to their actions.

In addition to its efforts on Capitol Hill, CUFI has also held meetings with senior officials in the Bush administration, such as one in 2006 with Deputy National Security Advisor Elliott Abrams that focused in part on Iran, and one this past fall, around the Annapolis peace conference, with National Security Advisor Stephen Hadley. In February, Hadley devoted a major portion of a speech at Stanford University to highlighting the continuing danger of the Iranian nuclear program. "The threat of a nuclear attack on the American homeland remains very real," he said, listing Iran as one of the sources of the threat.

For its part, AIPAC is behind an effort to tighten the financial noose around Tehran. Rather than pushing for wide-ranging sanctions, as some have in the past, AIPAC is lobbying lawmakers to introduce more specifically targeted—and potentially much more potent—sanctions, which may have a higher chance of being adopted than broader measures. While commending the latest U.N. sanctions, AIPAC is pushing for the U.S. government to unilaterally sanction "foreign banks who continue to conduct transactions with the four state-owned Iranian banks," and "designate the Central Bank of Iran as a supporter of terrorism and weapons proliferator," according to one of its recent policy memos.

In addition, according to AIPAC spokesman Josh Block, the organization is throwing its lobbying muscle behind two new congressional bills that include a raft of sharp measures—such as prohibiting foreign subsidiaries of U.S. companies from doing business with Iran. A key goal here is that the U.S. would no longer have to rely only on multilateral enforcement of U.N. sanctions to squeeze Iran. (AIPAC at this point is not advocating any military measures against Iran—arguably an untenable approach for any presidential contender if not most American politicians right now.)

McCain is a favorite of many in the AIPAC fold. Scheunemann, McCain's foreign policy director, also told me that McCain believes the new U.N. sanctions aren't enough, and that tougher measures are necessary. He said that McCain would support "sanctions outside of the U.N. framework," and that although "the military option is fraught with danger" he would not take it off the table.

It's possible that if Israel feels backed far enough into a corner, it may take matters into its own hands.

Propelled by Tehran's vitriolic words and increasing fears about its intentions, the Israeli government has been ratcheting up its own rhetoric in the wake of the NIE. A few weeks ago, Prime Minister Ehud Olmert was clear on his opinion of the situation. "The basic fact doesn't change. There is a plan to make non-conventional weapons and it must be stopped," he said. "Sometimes you don't need intelligence services. You just need to analyze what you know, what everyone knows, and it's very obvious and very simple."

When asked if this meant a military action was possible, Olmert used the line long heard from the Bush-Cheney White House. "No option is ruled out," he said.

It's possible that if Israel feels backed far enough into a corner, it may take matters into its own hands. "Planning for different scenarios—or intervention operations—has been under way for years," Ross, the former Mossad officer, told me. "And attempts have already been made. For example, attempts to shut off power grids to various installations."

There is an overwhelming consensus in the Israeli government, though, that any operation that went much beyond sabotage should be a last resort. From an Israeli point of view, it would be far preferable for the international community to do the dirty and dangerous work of defusing what is seen in Israel as a ticking Iranian bomb. This effort would presumably be led by the United States.

In "The Volunteer," a book about his experiences working for the Mossad, Ross recounts learning about Iran's intentions to gain nuclear weapons, long before it was such a big international issue. He told me he is certain that his successors in Israeli intelligence—as well as their colleagues in the Israeli diplomatic corps—are using regular liaison meetings with their U.S. counterparts to continually press for action against Iran. Because of this, he said, the release of the latest NIE, and the resulting weakening of the American stance, fueled a lot of anger among Israeli officials.

I asked him if he could foresee a time when Israel would lose faith that the international community or the United States would deal effectively with the Iranian situation, and decide to take action on its own. "It's in Israel's interest to squeeze as much as possible out of sanctions first," Ross said. "But I'm thinking that they're almost there anyway."

9

America Must be Prepared for a Possible Strike Against Iran

Patrick Clawson

Patrick Clawson is the deputy director for research of The Wash-
ington Institute for Near East Policy, as well as the author of
Forcing Hard Choices on Tehran, *coauthored with Michael*
Eisenstadt.

Given Iran's goal to become a nuclear power, it is time for the
United States to toughen its stance toward the country. The U.S.
must make clear that Iran has no chance of winning an arms
race, and that its neighbors should fear, not welcome, Iranian
nuclear weapons. America should also make plans for a pre-
emptive strike against Iran, and make plans for the aftermath of
a war, to not repeat the mistakes it committed during the Iraq
War.

The controversy over U.S. statements regarding Iranian arms in Iraq reflects the deep skepticism about how well the [George W.] Bush administration understands the world. The intelligence briefers in Baghdad got into trouble by making the natural human error of assuming that all right-thinking people would come to the same conclusion as they did after reviewing the evidence: since Iran's Al-Quds [elite guard] force is under the direct control of Iran's supreme religious leader and since senior Al-Quds officers were detained in Iraq carrying false identities and plans for attacking U.S. forces, then it must be the case that Iran's top leaders are behind the attacks on U.S. forces.

Patrick Clawson, "Iran Options," *The San Diego Union-Tribune*, February 18, 2007. Reproduced by permission of the author.

Likely? Yes. Proven? No. And making the claim has taken attention away from the well-established fact that sophisticated Iranian weapons are being used to kill American soldiers in Iraq.

Reliable Intelligence

In contrast to this overreaching, the U.S. approach to Iran's nuclear program has more often stuck to what can be completely proven. And that explains its greater success at building a broad international coalition and creating bipartisan support at home, compared to the skepticism about the Iraq claims. In December [2006], the United Nations Security Council unanimously—with Russia and China approving—voted to impose sanctions on Iran's dangerous nuclear "fuel cycle" activities. That came after three years of patient diplomacy concentrating on what is not in dispute, namely Iran's pursuit of a nuclear fuel cycle and its [eighteen] years of concealing its nuclear activities. Iran proudly trumpets its progress on the fuel cycle, giving tours of the massive facilities it is building. And Iran acknowledged that it hid its activities, claiming only that these were minor mistakes.

If the West hangs tough and steps up the pressure on Tehran, Iran may well in the end agree to suspend its nuclear program, though admittedly the near-term outlook is not good.

By concentrating on what is clearly established, Washington has been able to accomplish much more than if it had emphasized the intelligence that strongly suggests Iran already has an active nuclear weapons program. The international inspectors have found a lot of [suspect] indications Iran is working on a bomb, but there is no smoking gun. Explaining why to worry about Iran's nuclear fuel cycle is complicated; it is much simpler to warn that Iran is building a nuclear bomb.

But it is worth taking the extra effort to explain that if Iran completes the fuel cycle facilities it shows off to the world, then it will be on the brink of having a bomb. The Nobel Peace Prize-winning director general of the International Atomic Energy Agency, Mohammed El-Baradei—no fan of President George W. Bush—says that if Iran completes the facilities now being built, Tehran would be "a few months" away from having a bomb.

While the United States has been quite successful at building a broad coalition opposed to Iran's nuclear ambitions, Tehran continues to claim it is making great progress with its nuclear program. So has the U.S. effort been a triumph of appearance over substance? No, because the Iranian claim is not true: Iran has encountered many technical problems in its nuclear program, largely because it has been blocked from access to foreign assistance. The task now is to secure vigorous enforcement by all countries of Security Council Resolution 1737, which forbids Iranian access to dual-use technologies, that is, civilian technologies that can be applied to the nuclear program.

The Cold War offers instructive examples of how strong responses can bring better results.

Slowing Iran's Progress

The more Iran's nuclear program can be slowed, the more time for Iran's fundamental weaknesses and the West's abiding strengths to become apparent to the Islamic republic's hardline leaders, who have recently been overconfident because of temporary factors in their favor, such as a tight oil market and U.S. problems in Iraq. Already, the more business-minded Iranian leaders are realizing the high price that the country is paying for its nuclear program, especially since the U.S. Treasury has led a worldwide campaign to shut off Iran's access to international banks. A vigorous debate is occurring inside Iran about the wisdom of President Mahmoud Ahmadinejad's confrontational stances. If the West hangs tough and steps up the pressure on Tehran, Iran may well in the end agree to suspend its nuclear program, though admittedly the near-term outlook is not good.

In addition to pressing Iran, the United States needs to reassure its friends in the region that they are well protected against any threat from Iran. America does this not to be nice to oil-rich Arabs but because of U.S. interests in preventing Middle Eastern countries from starting their own nuclear programs. Nine regional countries—all U.S. allies, such as Turkey, Egypt, Saudi Arabia and the United Arab Emirates—have announced they are re-examining their nuclear options in reaction to the Iranian program. If all of them went the whole way to nuclear weapons, the world would be a much more dangerous place. The best way to forestall further nuclear proliferation is for the United States to take concrete steps to shore up the defenses against Iran. That explains why [in 2007] President [George W.] Bush ordered the deployment to the Persian Gulf of a second aircraft carrier and additional Patriot anti-missile defenses.

Echoes of the Cold War

One should hope the additional military assets sent to the Gulf will also persuade Iran's leaders that their nuclear program is hurting Iran's security by starting an arms build-up that will leave Iran worse off. The Cold War offers instructive examples of how strong responses can bring better results. When the Soviet Union deployed nuclear-tipped SS-20 missiles in Eastern Europe, NATO answered by stationing similar missiles in Western Europe, despite massive demonstrations against what protesters saw as [President Ronald] Reagan administration provocative saber-rattling. In fact, the NATO deployment dissuaded Moscow, which agreed to dismantle the SS-20s if NATO did the same to its missiles. We can hope that strong preparations to defend against Iranian nuclear-protected strong-arming of its neighbors will similarly dissuade Iran, such that Tehran agrees to stop its nuclear program in return for creation of a regional framework that protects Iran's security.

The second aircraft carrier deployed to the Gulf also increases the U.S. capability to pre-emptively strike Iranian nuclear facilities. But there are no reasons to carry out such a strike so long as Iran's nuclear program faces difficult technical barriers and diplomacy offers good prospects of resolving the crisis.

At the same time, the United States cannot rule out pre-emptive military force, because some in the Iranian revolutionary leadership with an apocalyptic world view might relish the opportunity to declare that Iran is about to explode a nuclear bomb, without clarifying if it was going to be inside Iran or on a Western or Israeli target. If they were to make such a threat, then pre-emptive military force would be well worth considering. Given that reality, the U.S. military certainly had better be preparing detailed plans now, so that America does not get caught flat-footed a la [as in] Iraq, not knowing what bad things could happen the day after the use of force. Such military planning would inevitably be misread by some as signs that an attack is near. But that is the price to be paid when so many in American society do not understand how the military works, including the importance of detailed contingency planning.

10

A Military Conflict with Iran Can Be Avoided

William Luers, Thomas Pickering, and Jim Walsh

William Luers is the president of the United Nations Association-USA and was formerly U.S. ambassador to Czechoslovakia and Venezuela. Thomas Pickering is co-chair of the United Nations Association-USA and the former undersecretary of state for political affairs. Jim Walsh is a research associate at the Massachusetts Institute of Technology.

Iran's strongest influence is felt in Iraq, where it provides insurgents with training and weapons. But Iran also supports militant organizations throughout the Middle East, and its influence cannot be underestimated.

Yet America cannot risk another cold war. Worsening relations between the United States and Iran will only lead to hostility and threaten the human rights situation. Talks with Iran on Iraq, Afghanistan, and the acquisition of nuclear power should lead to decreased hostility throughout the Middle East. Even though diplomacy might suffer temporary impasses, the United States must avoid a new cold war or another armed conflict in the region.

Three of the most pressing national security issues facing the [President Barack] Obama administration—nuclear proliferation, the war in Iraq, and the deteriorating situation in Afghanistan—have one element in common: Iran. The Islamic Republic has made startling progress over the past few years in its nuclear program. Setting aside recent, misleading reports that Iran already has enough nuclear fuel to build a weapon, the reality is that Tehran now has five thousand centrifuges for enriching uranium and is steadily moving toward achieving the capability to build nuclear bombs. Having the capacity to build a nuclear weapon is not the same thing as having one, and having a large stock of low-enriched uranium is not the same as having the highly enriched uranium necessary for a bomb. But the Obama administration cannot postpone dealing with the nuclear situation in Iran, as President [George W.] Bush did.

Iran is closely implicated in the conflicts in Iraq and Afghanistan as well. Iran's influence in Iraq is well known. As Michael Massing [a contributing editor of the *Columbia Journalism Review*] has reported . . .:

> The SIIC [Supreme Islamic Iraqi Council], the main government party, was founded in Iran and remains so close to Tehran that many Iraqis shun it for having a "Persian taint." Iran is erecting mosques and power plants in the Shiite south and investing heavily in construction and communications in the Kurdish north.

Under President [George W.] Bush, Iran's nuclear program and its role in Iraq and Afghanistan were treated as wholly separate issues.

Iran's Expanding Influence

But Iran also has critical interests in Afghanistan, its neighbor to the east, where it has long opposed the Taliban and is concerned to avoid the chaos that would result from the fall of the increasingly threatened [Hamid] Karzai government. The Iranian government places a high priority on defeating al-Qaeda and the Taliban—extremist Sunni [Islamic denomination] groups which it views as direct threats to Iran's Shiites [Islamic denomination]—as well as on reducing Afghanistan's rampant drug trade.

Of course the United States has other important concerns about Iran, including Iranian support for Hezbollah [a Shia Islamist political and paramilitary organization based in Lebanon] and Hamas [a Palestinian sociopolitical, militant organization], and the threat it poses to Israel—particularly in view of the recent conflict in Gaza. But the paramount issues of Iran's nuclear enrichment and its influence in Iraq and Afghanistan, we argue, are closely interrelated, and the way they are dealt with could determine the US's ability to address other problems in the US–Iranian relationship.

Under President [George W.] Bush, Iran's nuclear program and its role in Iraq and Afghanistan were treated as wholly separate issues. The US government largely refused to talk to Iran on the nuclear issue and instead relied on sanctions and hectoring. By contrast, on the issue of Iraq, it agreed to ambassadorial talks, although these were largely limited to discussions of Iraq's internal security issues, including Iranian provision of weapons to insurgents. On Afghanistan, aside from occasional allegations about collaboration with the Taliban—this despite Iran's well-known opposition to the group—the Bush administration studiously ignored Iran. As a consequence, little progress was made on any front.

If President Obama is to dissuade Iran from building a nuclear bomb, as well as develop a successful regional strategy in Iraq and Afghanistan, he will have to develop an integrated approach toward Iran that addresses all three issues.

First, both sides must recognize the connection among these issues. Success with one can build trust and create confidence needed for progress on the others. Failure on one could stymie [halt] advancement on the others. Using military force against Iran's nuclear facilities, for example, would make cooperation on Iraq and Afghanistan impossible. Discussions across a broader agenda also create opportunities for constructive compromise. A concession on one issue can be used to resolve a sticking point on another.

Resolving the nuclear issue and bringing stability to Iraq and Afghanistan will require direct talks between the United States, Iran, and other interested parties, and these talks must be without preconditions.

Building Consensus

Second, for such a strategy to work the US must consult in advance other parties including, most particularly, the other four permanent members of the UN [United Nations] Security Council (France, Britain, Russia, and China), the UN secretary-general, Israel, Turkey, Pakistan, and the Arab countries. The governments in the region have a direct interest in Iran's nuclear program, the future of Iraq and Afghanistan, and US–Iranian relations. All of the countries listed have a stake in one or more of these issues, and success is more likely if they believe their concerns are being taken into account, not excluded.

The third requirement of an integrated strategy would be to create a continuing forum or other institution that would allow the US, Iran, members of the Security Council, and neighboring governments to discuss questions involving Iraq and Afghanistan. No such institution now exists.

Resolving the nuclear issue and bringing stability to Iraq and Afghanistan will require direct talks between the United States, Iran, and other interested parties, and these talks must be without preconditions. President-elect Obama has pledged to do just that. Still, for a government to say that it is ready for talks is not enough. Three issues must be addressed before proceeding: when to talk, what to say, and how to say it.

Even if the pace of confirmation hearings and security clearances is uncharacteristically swift, it will be at least several months before the President's foreign policy team is ready to advance a major shift in policy toward Iran. By that time, Iran will be in the middle of the campaign for its June 12 [2009] presidential elections. That vote will likely be followed by a run-off election held later in the summer.

We suggest that a new policy be launched after the new Iranian president is chosen. A major diplomatic initiative begun in the middle of Iran's presidential campaign would almost certainly become caught up in Iran's domestic politics with consequences that are difficult to predict. The administration can use this time to win the support of members of Congress as well as the Europeans, Russians, and Chinese who have been part of the so-called "P5+1" talks with Iran—involving the five permanent members of the UN Security Council plus Germany.

A Dialogue with Iran

Equally if not more important, the Obama administration will have to consult with and reassure the US's friends and allies in the region—notably the Arab states, Turkey, Pakistan, and Israel. It will have to make ... clear that a dialogue with Iran does not mean a downgrading of our relations with other Muslim countries in the region, and that America's direct engagement with Iran serves their security and political interests, for example, by diplomatically resolving issues that might otherwise lead to the use of American (or Israeli) military force. As regards Israel, the US should emphasize that engaging Iran offers the best chance of heading off an Iranian nuclear weapons program and for dealing with the threat Israel faces from Hezbollah and Hamas.

While the Obama administration prepares for a major diplomatic push following the Iranian elections, it should take a number of actions in the meantime. These actions would be modest and low-key but would send an unambiguous signal to the Iranian government that the US is prepared to enter serious negotiations at the appropriate time. Early on, the Obama administration could offer a simple statement that the US government will seek to talk directly to all nations, without preconditions, in order to address the world's problems. This could be followed by a reaffirmation of Article I of the 1981 Algiers Accord, in which the United States pledged not to interfere politically or militarily in Iran's internal affairs.

Iran is a proud nation with roots in a centuries-old civilization; its insistence on being treated with mutual respect is not empty rhetoric.

Following these initial actions and before the results of the Iranian presidential elections become apparent, the US should consider opening mid-level, official contact with Iran to discuss simultaneous public actions that each government could take to improve the tone and, eventually, the substance of the relationship. This direct contact could explore renewed talks on Iraq, releasing Iranian detainees captured in Iraq, allowing direct air flights between the US and Iran, easing travel restrictions on Iranian diplomats in New York, the establishment of a US-staffed interests section in Tehran, new forms of cooperation to combat illicit drug trafficking on the Afghan–Iranian border, and confidence-building measures among the two countries' naval forces in the Persian Gulf. (As it stands, the US and Iran find themselves cheek to jowl both in the Persian Gulf and along the Iraq–Iran border—a dangerous situation that risks accident, escalating tensions, or even war.)

Actions such as these are limited in scope, and would not at first substantively alter the character of US–Iranian relations, but they would communicate to Iran that the US intends to pursue a different strategy from the one followed by the previous administration. Following the Iranian elections in the summer, the new administration could privately and informally explore the idea of talks at a higher level.

Shutting Up

A new policy also requires a new tone. Iran is a proud nation with roots in a centuries-old civilization; its insistence on being treated with mutual respect is not empty rhetoric. Continued denunciation of the regime will likely produce greater intransigence, especially as Iran enters its presidential campaign. Iranians bristle at the use of the phrase "carrots and sticks," which they associate with the treatment of donkeys and which in any case suggests that they can be either bought off or beaten into submission. More generally, the US government would do well to follow a first principle of diplomacy—when you want to change a bad situation, start by shutting up.

Moreover, Iranian paranoia about the US cannot be underestimated. Alerting the Iranian government in advance to the timing and objectives of each of the steps described above would avoid a negative reaction. It would also prepare the way for a major new approach to the issues concerning nuclear enrichment, Iraq, and Afghanistan. . . .

We have proposed that the United States engage in direct, bilateral talks with Iran on its nuclear program in parallel with continued multilateral discussions with Germany and the members of the UN Security Council (the "P5+1"). We envisage a prominent role for America's European partners in the establishment of a multilateral enrichment facility on Iranian soil. We believe that this approach offers crucial advantages not only for the nuclear issue but for addressing the parallel challenges of Iraq and Afghanistan. Here again, we argue that the US and Iran should hold separate but parallel direct discussions on the issues of Iraq and Afghanistan, and that these discussions, in turn, must become part of a broader, multiparty approach that includes the members of the Security Council and neighboring countries in the region. On the US side, these three distinct but related tracks would be coordinated by the secretary of state.

Exploratory negotiations in the region will first require a solution to the problem of who will participate and how best to coordinate their relations. Each major issue—Iraq, Afghanistan, and the Iran nuclear problem—would have its own negotiating forum, or track, with Iran and the other key players participating. Working in parallel with the UN secretary-general, an umbrella group, including all the major players, would be established to coordinate the work of the smaller groups and ratify the results.

As far as Iraq is concerned, in Washington's ideal world, Tehran would have no influence over Iraqi affairs, and Iraq would act as a stalwart supporter of American interests and allies in the region. Tehran would like the same for itself, namely, an Iraq over which America has little or no influence and an Iraqi government dominated by Shiite factions friendly to Iranian interests. Despite these differences, there is much on which the US and Iran can agree. Both support keeping Iraq territorially intact (rather than carved up into separate, sectarian regions) and with popularly elected leadership.

Neither the US nor Iran is likely to achieve all of its aims in Iraq.

Common Ground

Indeed, although Iran has shown its readiness to support militias that attack US troops, both countries support the Maliki government [in Iraq], and neither wants to see Iraq become the battleground for proxy [substitute] wars, in which neighboring countries provide military or political support for their client groups inside Iraq. Saudi Arabia, for example, might increase its support for Sunni tribal groups such as those in [Iraq's] Anbar province—which continue to be regarded with deep suspicion by the Maliki government—while Iran might feel compelled to bolster Shiite militias or elements in the Iraqi security forces. The aim of negotiations would be to avoid both kinds of intervention.

The United States wants to be able to draw down troops and other personnel in Iraq while maintaining a reasonable level of stability and security. Iran also wants US forces out of Iraq, while avoiding a situation of renewed chaos and civil war. Iran also has economic interests in Iraq, which it sees as a potential trading partner and OPEC [Organization of the Petroleum Exporting Countries] ally.

Neither the US nor Iran is likely to achieve all of its aims in Iraq. For the US, it is a stubborn and unalterable fact of geography that while its forces may leave Iraq, Iran will always be there, sharing a border with its neighbor and sometime rival. On the other hand, Iraq will likely want to maintain a relationship with the US, if only to counterbalance Iran's influence. Most Iraqi Shias, despite common religious preferences and temporary connections with Iran, have no interest in becoming Persian puppets.

Both the US and Iran would profit if they were willing to settle for a stable and secure Iraq to which both countries have strong ties but over which neither is dominant. The stakes are sufficiently high and the potential for disastrous conflict sufficiently strong that there is reason to find common ground on mutual interests. . . .

Brokering Peace in Iraq

The diplomatic effort proposed here would have several components. First, the US president would appoint a special envoy to initiate a round of diplomacy with all the governments in the region to address questions concerning Iraq. The UN secretary-general would designate a diplomatic team that would work in parallel with or together with the US special envoy to establish such a team. The US, together with the other permanent members of the UN Security Council and Iraq's neighbors, would share the burden in organizing this initiative. American leadership will be critical, but Washington cannot monopolize the effort. If it does, this will be perceived as yet another "Made in the USA" project imposed from outside and intended to further American interests at the expense of others. International participation under UN auspices will provide the kind of legitimacy needed for the project to succeed.

A priority for the UN and the US envoys would be to make it clear to Baghdad that the first and most important goal of this initiative is the support of Iraqi sovereignty and regional stability and that any decisions or actions would be consistent with the objectives of the Iraqis themselves. This is important, because no plan for Iraq can succeed without the support of the Iraqis. At the same time, no such plan can succeed—even if it has the support of Iraq and its Sunni neighbors—without the endorsement and participation of Iran.

The forum would have both near-term and long-term objectives. At the beginning, the UN and US envoys would meet with participating governments bilaterally with the goal of agreeing to refrain from interfering with or undermining the government of Iraq. The forum would also allow Iraq's neighbors to articulate to international negotiators their suspicions and grievances about the behavior of others in the region and have them addressed. These UN-endorsed exploratory exchanges can also be used to better coordinate the material and political support that the regional and great power governments are providing to Iraq.

The long-term objective might be a formal agreement in which all participating governments pledge themselves to a set of principles and actions: supporting Iraq's territorial integrity, encouraging reconciliation between the various groups within Iraq (based on majority rule, minority rights, and the fair division of oil income), abstaining from interference in Iraqi internal affairs, ending military support for non-state groups operating in Iraq, planning for the resettlement of the five million Iraqis who have been displaced from their homes, whether outside or inside Iraq, bolstering economic and political relations between Iraq and its neighbors, and the inclusion of Iraq in any future regional security arrangements. These resolutions will be of particular importance to Iran, because Tehran wants a stable and friendly neighbor on its border—one governed by Iraq's Shia majority and without a large contingent of US troops on its territory. In addition, Iran's interest in Iraq's economic development will continue to be substantial. Iran has benefited in the past from trade with Iraq but has suffered when Iraq has been unstable or aggressively hostile, as under Saddam Hussein.

Afghanistan and its increasingly volatile neighbor, Pakistan, face deeply difficult problems, many of which now threaten to engulf the entire region.

All the governments in the Middle East have a common interest in avoiding wholesale disintegration and civil war in the region, but it would be naive to think that there are not obstacles or risks associated with this approach. The Saudis, for example, support Sunni militias against what they see as Shia retribution. Saudi Arabia has less leverage in Iraq than Iran [does] and worries that Iran's star is ascending. Like other Sunni countries, Saudi Arabia also views the Maliki government as unfriendly. Turkey's leaders fear that the good relations that the Shias of Iraq and Iran have established with the Iraqi Kurds will bring about their worst nightmare—a declared and recognized independent Kurdistan. This is a result Turkey cannot accept, despite the fact that the Kurdish population has explicitly supported it.

A Multilateral Approach Is Needed

There are obvious risks to what we propose. Not only may a multilateral initiative for Iraq fail, but a regional forum could become an arena where disputing parties seek to frustrate or dominate others. While this is one potential outcome, we believe the risks are far greater if the countries continue to pursue their current, independent policies in Iraq. Without an institution that allows for the recognition and management of their competing interests, the parties will act on their own, and the results will play out in the streets of Kirkuk and Baghdad. Finally, it is almost certain that there will be increased suspicion and rivalry between the United States and Iran if Iran is left to pursue its own interests in Iraq without some form of regional mediation. Each side will see the worst in the other and publicly blame the other for rising violence and dislocation—including, for example, the recent dramatic escalation of the conflict between Israel and Hamas in Gaza. In this context of deepening anger and distrust, it will be even more difficult to address other issues the US and Iran should be discussing, such as the future of Afghanistan and Iran's nuclear program.

Afghanistan and its increasingly volatile neighbor, Pakistan, face deeply difficult problems, many of which now threaten to engulf the entire region. Having been given sanctuary in northwest Pakistan after September 11 [2001], the Taliban have very substantially increased their presence in Afghanistan, while Pakistan itself has become a safe haven for al-Qaeda and other terrorist organizations, including those that attacked Mumbai [Indian City, formerly known as Bombay] in December [2008].

These developments are of great concern to Iran, which shares borders with both Afghanistan and Pakistan. In fact, Iran supported Northern Alliance forces against the Taliban, and contributed in important ways to the overthrow of the Taliban regime in 2001. Renewed Iranian assistance, for example in the form of political cooperation, could help prevent the continued spread of the conflict. The Afghanistan expert Barney Rubin has pointed out that US–Iranian cooperation will be crucial for the Afghanistan presidential elections to be held in the second half of this year [2009]. If an election is not possible, the US will again need Iran's help to organize a Loya Jirga (a traditional assembly of tribal leaders used in Afghanistan to resolve important political matters), drawing on Iran's longstanding ties and influence over some Afghan warlords and tribal leaders.

The US can impose costs on Iran, but it cannot impose its will.

Time Is Running Out

A US decision on a new strategy toward Iran will not wait. That is President-elect Obama's inheritance. Talking to Iran will be difficult. In the US, some political leaders and interest groups oppose better relations, though public opinion surveys suggest that a solid majority of Americans favor a diplomatic solution to US–Iranian differences over nuclear enrichment and other issues. Similarly, in Iran, an attempt to engage or compromise with the US will be attacked by factions seeking a political advantage, despite the hopes of millions of Iranians that the US and Iran find a way to improve relations. Suspicion dominates a relationship with a long history of grievances on both sides. Washington doubts the innocence of Iran's nuclear intentions, and Tehran suspects that America's real intent is regime change.

Moreover, some analysts, including many Israelis, view Iran as an "existential threat" to Israel, object to Iran's backing of Hezbollah, and believe that Iran's support for Hamas undermines a two-state solution between Israel and Palestine. In addition, Iran's human rights record provokes understandable opposition internationally. These concerns are extremely urgent, but deteriorating relations between Washington and Tehran will only strengthen Iranian hard-liners and therefore exacerbate the human rights situation. US–Iranian hostility may also give Iran a greater incentive to exercise its leverage with Hamas and Hezbollah in ways that undermine a resolution to the Israel-Palestinian dispute. We believe that successful engagement with Iran on Iraq, Afghanistan, and the nuclear issue could translate into progress on other issues. Indeed, Iran's secret 2003 proposal for US talks included on its agenda Hamas, Hezbollah, and a two-state solution.

The US can impose costs on Iran, but it cannot impose its will. The same is true for Iran. Progress requires on both sides a greater focus on strategy rather than tactics. Adopting a new, integrated approach will require political leadership that is disciplined and willing to take risks. There could be frustrations, setbacks, and dangers, but the US and Iran can avoid a downward spiral that risks military conflict. They can also create an opportunity for progress on some of the most difficult and complicated challenges the US will have to confront in the coming years.

11

America Must Bomb Iran to Answer Its Nuclear and Terrorist Threat

Norman Podhoretz

Norman Podhoretz is editor-at-large of Commentary, *and the author of* World War IV: The Long Struggle Against Islamofascism.

America is currently at war with Iran and its Islamofascism, a totalitarianism on par with Hitler's Third Reich and the Cold War Soviet Union. Diplomacy never worked with Adolf Hitler, and it has not worked since. Neither have sanctions imposed against fascist regimes. The only option for the United States is a military strike against Iran.

Although many persist in denying it, I continue to believe that what Sept. 11, 2001, did was to plunge us headlong into nothing less than another world war. I call this new war World War IV, because I also believe that what is generally known as the Cold War was actually World War III, and that this one bears a closer resemblance to that great conflict than it does to World War II. Like the Cold War, as the military historian Eliot Cohen was the first to recognize, the one we are now in has ideological roots, pitting us against Islamofascism, yet another mutation of the totalitarian disease we defeated first in the shape of Nazism and fascism and then in the shape of communism; it is global in scope; it is being fought with a variety of weapons, not all of them military; and it is likely to go on for decades.

A New Global Struggle

What follows from this way of looking at the last five years is that the military campaigns in Afghanistan and Iraq cannot be understood if they are regarded as self-contained wars in their own right. Instead we have to see them as fronts or theaters that have been opened up in the early stages of a protracted global struggle. The same thing is true of Iran. As the currently main center of the Islamofascist ideology against which we have been fighting since 9/11, and as (according to the State Department's latest annual report on the subject) the main sponsor of the terrorism that is Islamofascism's weapon of choice, Iran too is a front in World War IV. Moreover, its effort to build a nuclear arsenal makes it the potentially most dangerous one of all.

The Iranians, of course, never cease denying that they intend to build a nuclear arsenal, and yet in the same breath they openly tell us what they intend to do with it. Their first priority, as repeatedly and unequivocally announced by their president, Mahmoud Ahmadinejad, is to "wipe Israel off the map"—a feat that could not be accomplished by conventional weapons alone.

But Ahmadinejad's ambitions are not confined to the destruction of Israel. He also wishes to dominate the greater Middle East, and thereby to control the oilfields of the region and the flow of oil out of it through the Persian Gulf. If he acquired a nuclear capability, he would not even have to use it in order to put all this within his reach. Intimidation and blackmail by themselves would do the trick.

Nor are Ahmadinejad's ambitions merely regional in scope. He has a larger dream of extending the power and influence of Islam throughout Europe, and this too he hopes to accomplish by playing on the fear that resistance to Iran would lead to a nuclear war. And then, finally, comes the largest dream of all: what Ahmadinejad does not shrink from describing as "a world without America." Demented though he may be, I doubt that Ahmadinejad is so crazy as to imagine that he could wipe America off the map even if he had nuclear weapons. But what he probably does envisage is a diminution of the American will to oppose him: that is, if not a world without America, he will settle, at least in the short run, for a world without much American influence. . . .

The Iranians, of course, never cease denying that they intend to build a nuclear arsenal, and yet in the same breath they openly tell us what they intend to do with it.

The Alternatives to Military Intervention

But if military force is ruled out, what is supposed to do the job?

Well, to begin with, there is that good old standby, diplomacy. And so, for 3 1/2 years, even predating the accession [rise] of Ahmadinejad to the presidency, the diplomatic gavotte [type of dance] has been danced with Iran, in negotiations whose carrot-and-stick details no one can remember— not even, I suspect, the parties involved. But since, to say it again, Ahmadinejad is a revolutionary with unlimited aims and not a statesman with whom we can "do business," all this negotiating has had the same result as Munich had with Hitler. That is, it has bought the Iranians more time in which they have moved closer and closer to developing nuclear weapons.

Then there are sanctions. As it happens, sanctions have very rarely worked in the past. Worse yet, they have usually ended up hurting the hapless people of the targeted country while leaving the leadership unscathed. Nevertheless, much hope has been invested in them as a way of bringing Ahmadinejad to heel. Yet thanks to the resistance of Russia and China, both of which have reasons of their own to go easy on Iran, it has proved enormously difficult for the [United Nations] Security Council to impose sanctions that could even conceivably be effective. At first, the only measures to which Russia and China would agree were much too limited even to bite. Then, as Iran continued to defy Security Council resolutions and to block inspections by the International Atomic Energy Agency [IAEA] that it was bound by treaty to permit, not even the Russians and the Chinese were able to hold out against stronger sanctions. Once more, however, these have had little or no effect on the progress Iran is making toward the development of a nuclear arsenal. On the contrary: they, too, have bought the Iranians additional time in which to move ahead.

Since hope springs eternal, some now believe that the answer lies in more punishing sanctions. This time, however, their purpose would be not to force Iran into compliance, but to provoke an internal uprising against Ahmadinejad and the regime as a whole. Those who advocate this course tell us that the "mullocracy" [after "mullah," the religious leaders] is very unpopular, especially with young people, who make up a majority of Iran's population. They tell us that these young people would like nothing better than to get rid of the oppressive and repressive and corrupt regime under which they now live and to replace it with a democratic system. And they tell us, finally, that if Iran were so transformed, we would have nothing to fear from it even if it were to acquire nuclear weapons.

As it happens, sanctions have very rarely worked in the past.

Once upon a time, under the influence of Bernard Lewis [professor of Near Eastern studies emeritus at Princeton University] and others I respect, I too subscribed to this school of thought. But after three years and more of waiting for the insurrection they assured us back then was on the verge of erupting, I have lost confidence in their prediction. Some of them blame the [George W.] Bush administration for not doing enough to encourage an uprising, which is why they have now transferred their hopes to sanctions that would inflict so much damage on the Iranian economy that the entire populace would rise up against the rulers. Yet whether or not this might happen under such circumstances, there is simply no chance of getting Russia and China, or the Europeans for that matter, to agree to the kind of sanctions that are the necessary precondition.

Why Diplomacy Won't Work

At the outset I stipulated that the weapons with which we are fighting World War IV are not all military—that they also include economic, diplomatic, and other nonmilitary instruments of power. In exerting pressure for reform on countries like Egypt and Saudi Arabia, these nonmilitary instruments are the right ones to use. But it should be clear by now to any observer not in denial that Iran is not such a country. As we know from Iran's defiance of the Security Council and the IAEA even while the United States has been warning Ahmadinejad that "all options" remain on the table, ultimatums and threats of force can no more stop him than negotiations and sanctions have managed to do. Like them, all they accomplish is to buy him more time.

In short, the plain and brutal truth is that if Iran is to be prevented from developing a nuclear arsenal, there is no alternative to the actual use of military force—any more than there was an alternative to force if Hitler was to be stopped in 1938.

Since a ground invasion of Iran must be ruled out for many different reasons, the job would have to be done, if it is to be done at all, by a campaign of air strikes. Furthermore, because Iran's nuclear facilities are dispersed, and because some of them are underground, many sorties and bunker-busting munitions would be required. And because such a campaign is beyond the capabilities of Israel, and the will, let alone the courage, of any of our other allies, it could be carried out only by the United States. Even then, we would probably be unable to get at all the underground facilities, which means that, if Iran were still intent on going nuclear, it would not have to start over again from scratch. But a bombing campaign would without question set back its nuclear program for years to come, and might even lead to the overthrow of the mullahs.

The plain and brutal truth is that if Iran is to be prevented from developing a nuclear arsenal, there is no alternative to the actual use of military force.

The opponents of bombing—not just the usual suspects but many both here and in Israel who have no illusions about the nature and intentions and potential capabilities of the Iranian regime—disagree that it might end in the overthrow of the mullocracy. On the contrary, they are certain that all Iranians, even the democratic dissidents, would be impelled to rally around the flag. And this is only one of the worst-case scenarios they envisage. To wit: Iran would retaliate by increasing the trouble it is already making for us in Iraq. It would attack Israel with missiles armed with nonnuclear warheads but possibly containing biological or chemical weapons. There would be a vast increase in the price of oil, with catastrophic consequences for every economy in the world, very much including our own. The worldwide outcry against the inevitable civilian casualties would make the anti-Americanism of today look like a lovefest.

Bombing Iran Is the Only Solution

I readily admit that it would be foolish to discount any or all of these scenarios. Each of them is, alas, only too plausible. Nevertheless, there is a good response to them, and it is the one given by [Senator] John McCain. The only thing worse than bombing Iran, McCain has declared, is allowing Iran to get the bomb.

And yet those of us who agree with McCain are left with the question of whether there is still time. If we believe the Iranians, the answer is no. In early April [2007], at Iran's Nuclear Day festivities, Ahmadinejad announced that the point of no return in the nuclearization process had been reached. If this is true, it means that Iran is only a small step away from producing nuclear weapons. But even supposing that Ahmadinejad is bluffing, in order to convince the world that it is already too late to stop him, how long will it take before he actually turns out to have a winning hand?

If we believe the CIA, perhaps as much as 10 years. But CIA estimates have so often been wrong that they are hardly more credible than the boasts of Ahmadinejad. Other estimates by other experts fall within the range of a few months to six years. Which is to say that no one really knows. And because no one really knows, the only prudent—indeed, the only *responsible*—course is to assume that Ahmadinejad may not be bluffing, or may only be exaggerating a bit, and to strike at him as soon as it is logistically possible.

In his 2002 State of the Union address, President Bush made a promise:

> We'll be deliberate, yet time is not on our side. I will not wait on events, while dangers gather. I will not stand by, as peril draws closer and closer. The United States of America will not permit the world's most dangerous regimes to threaten us with the world's most destructive weapons.

In that speech, the president was referring to Iraq, but he has made it clear on a number of subsequent occasions that the same principle applies to Iran. Indeed, he has gone so far as to say that if we permit Iran to build a nuclear arsenal, people 50 years from now will look back and wonder how we of this generation could have allowed such a thing to happen, and they will rightly judge us as harshly as we today judge the British and the French for what they did and what they failed to do at Munich in 1938. I find it hard to understand why George W. Bush would have put himself so squarely in the dock of history on this issue if he were resigned to leaving office with Iran in possession of nuclear weapons, or with the ability to build them. Accordingly, my guess is that he intends, within the next 21 months, to order air strikes against the Iranian nuclear facilities from the three U.S. aircraft carriers already sitting nearby.

The only thing worse than bombing Iran ... is allowing Iran to get the bomb.

"Giving Futility Its Chance"

But if that is what he has in mind, why is he spending all this time doing the diplomatic dance and wasting so much energy on getting the Russians and the Chinese to sign on to sanctions? The reason, I suspect, is that—to borrow a phrase from [American historian] Robert Kagan —he has been "giving futility its chance." Not that this is necessarily a cynical ploy. For it may well be that he has entertained the remote possibility of a diplomatic solution under which Iran would follow the example of Libya in voluntarily giving up its nuclear program. Besides, once having played out the diplomatic string, and thereby having demonstrated that to him force is truly a last resort, Mr. Bush would be in a stronger political position to endorse John McCain's formula that the only thing worse than bombing Iran would be allowing Iran to build a nuclear bomb—and not just to endorse that assessment, but to act on it.

If this is what Mr. Bush intends to do, it goes, or should go, without saying that his overriding purpose is to ensure the security of this country in accordance with the vow he took upon becoming president, and in line with his pledge not to stand by while one of the world's most dangerous regimes threatens us with one of the world's most dangerous weapons.

But there is, it has been reported, another consideration that is driving Mr. Bush. According to a recent news story in the *New York Times*, for example, Bush has taken to heart what "officials from 21 governments in and around the Middle East warned at a meeting of Arab leaders in March"—namely, "that Iran's drive for atomic technology could result in the beginning of 'a grave and destructive nuclear arms race in the region.'" Which is to say that he fears that local resistance to Iran's bid for hegemony [predominance] in the greater Middle East through the acquisition of nuclear weapons could have even more dangerous consequences than a passive capitulation to that bid by the Arab countries. For resistance would spell the doom of all efforts to stop the spread of nuclear weapons, and it would vastly increase the chances of their use.

Avoiding a New Holocaust

I have no doubt that this ominous prospect figures prominently in the president's calculations. But it seems evident to me that the survival of Israel, a country to which George W. Bush has been friendlier than any president before him, is also of major concern to him—a concern fully coincident with his worries over a Middle Eastern arms race.

Much of the world has greeted Ahmadinejad's promise to wipe Israel off the map with something close to insouciance [indifference]. In fact, it could almost be said of the Europeans that they have been more upset by Ahmadinejad's denial that a Holocaust took place 60 years ago than by his determination to set off one of his own as soon as he acquires the means to do so. In some ... European countries, Holocaust denial is a crime, and the European Union only recently endorsed that position. Yet for all their retrospective remorse over the wholesale slaughter of Jews back then, the Europeans seem no readier to lift a finger to prevent a second Holocaust than they were the first time around.

Not so George W. Bush, a man who knows evil when he sees it and who has demonstrated an unfailingly courageous willingness to endure vilification [smear] and contumely [harsh language] in setting his face against it. It now remains to be seen whether this president, battered more mercilessly and with less justification than any other in living memory, and weakened politically by the enemies of his policy in the Middle East in general and Iraq in particular, will find it possible to take the only action that can stop Iran from following through on its evil intentions both toward us and toward Israel. As an American and as a Jew, I pray with all my heart that he will.

12

Military Action Cannot Solve the Problems with Iran

Barbara Slavin

Barbara Slavin is assistant managing editor for world and national security at the Washington Times. *She is the author of* Bitter Friends, Bosom Enemies: Iran, the U.S. and the Twisted Path to Confrontation.

Iran has once again become a country of great political influence in the Middle East, and the Bush administration's inflammatory rhetoric has done nothing to further talks between Washington and Tehran. Military action cannot solve the challenge Iran poses to U.S. interests. It won't eradicate the nuclear program, and it will foster hostility against America in the region. Iran is much more open to talks than is currently believed, and only negotiations between the two countries will lead to lasting peace.

With America's intervention in Iraq facing such uncertain prospects, starting a new war in the Middle East would seem the epitome [model] of folly. Yet talk of attacking Iran keeps bubbling up in Washington—and not just among the neoconservatives who promoted the war in Iraq. President [George W.] Bush, many Republicans have told me, will not feel comfortable leaving office with Iran continuing to install and spin centrifuges. Having vowed that he would not permit the world's most dangerous regimes to possess the world's most dangerous weapons, Bush worries that his legacy will be faulted even more for failure to contain Iran than for the carnage he unleashed in Iraq.

Barbara Slavin, "Negotiation, Not War: How to Deal with Iran," *Encyclopædia Britannica Blog*, October 10, 2007. Reprinted with permission from *Encyclopædia Britannica Blog*, © 2007 by Encyclopædia Britannica, Inc.

Bush has reason to be concerned. Iran has made considerable progress toward a bomb on his watch. Even if Iran never tests a nuclear weapon, the belief that it is capable of building one would embolden it and militant groups it supports, such as Hezbollah [a Shia Islamist political and paramilitary organization in Lebanon] and Hamas [a Palestinian, sociopolitical, militant movement]. Iran's neighbors, particularly Saudi Arabia, would likely seek nuclear weapons. Israel would be especially unnerved, given Iranian President Mahmoud Ahmadinejad's "wipe Israel off the map" rhetoric. Former Israeli deputy Defense Minister Ephraim Sneh has warned that it would be harder to attract Jewish immigrants to Israel given the existential threat a nuclear Iran would pose.

A Military Strike Would Not Stop the Nuclear Program

Yet attacking Iran, while it might retard the nuclear program by a few years, would hardly end it. It is only prudent—given the track record of U.S. intelligence—to assume that Iran has facilities that the CIA knows nothing about. And 1,000-pound bombs cannot destroy the knowledge in the heads of Iran's nuclear scientists.

Meanwhile, the collateral damage would be devastating. The price of oil would leap over $100 a barrel, plunging much of the world into recession. Iran-backed groups would intensify attacks on American troops still in Iraq. Iran would encourage its other proxies [substitutes] to attack U.S. targets and might feel justified in doing something it has never done before—striking Americans in our homeland. Al-Qaeda, finally on the defensive in Iraq as Sunni tribesmen rise up against it, would be thrilled to see its two worst enemies—Americans and Shiites—come to blows and would gain new fodder for recruitment. Much of the non-Muslim world would also decry U.S. action, given the fact that Iran does not yet possess nuclear weapons and claims that it has no intention of building them.

What then should the United States do to stop Iran from becoming the world's tenth nuclear weapons state? Before it can come up with an honest answer to that question, the White House might start by admitting—at least to itself—that its own policies, as well as those of previous administrations, were at least partly to blame.

Attacking Iran, while it might retard the nuclear program by a few years, would hardly end it.

Before the 1979 Islamic revolution, both Democratic and Republican administrations encouraged Iran to have nuclear power. Iran got its first research reactor from [President] Lyndon Johnson. Under the [President Gerald] Ford administration—when Dick Cheney was White House chief of staff and Donald Rumsfeld was on his first stint as Defense Secretary—Iran contracted to buy eight U.S. reactors. Following the overthrow of the Shah, U.S. companies cancelled the contracts and U.S. administrations tried to convince other countries not to export nuclear technology to Iran.

The Nuclear Black Market

Much of what Iran knows about uranium enrichment appears to have come from the black market run by Pakistan's A.Q. Khan. But in deciding to invade Iraq—the one member of the "Axis of Evil" that no longer had an advanced nuclear program—the Bush administration spurred Iran to redouble efforts to master uranium enrichment. Robert Hutchings, who from 2003–2005 headed the National Intelligence Council, the board that prepares intelligence estimates for the White House, said the council warned in early 2003 that as a result of the U.S. pursuit of regime change in Iraq, "the Iranian regime, like the North Korean regime, would probably judge that their best option would be to acquire nuclear weapons as fast as possible because the possession of nuclear weapons offers protection" from U.S. attack.

Doomed Negotiations

The [George W.] Bush administration has also missed repeated opportunities for negotiations with Iran that might have persuaded it to abandon or at least limit its nuclear ambitions. Assuming victory in Iraq, the U.S. rejected an authoritative Iranian offer for talks in May 2003 on all the issues dividing the two countries. In 2006, the White House also refused requests for back-channel talks with a deputy to Iranian national security adviser Ali Larijani. In May last year [2006], the administration belatedly agreed to negotiate, provided Iran first suspended uranium enrichment. But U.S. policy continues to be undercut by strategic confusion. The White House wants to have it both ways—attacking the legitimacy of the government it wants to disarm. Why on earth should Tehran give up a possible deterrent against U.S. attack while Bush pledges "to stand with" the people of Iran if they rise up against their regime?

After six years of faith-based foreign policy, a dose of Nixonian realpolitik [political pragmatism] might be in order. The Bush administration must be willing to negotiate with Tehran without preconditions—as it has recently with North Korea—as other administrations have done in the past. When they met Zhou Enlai and Mao Tsetung in 1972, Henry Kissinger and Richard Nixon did not urge the people of China to overthrow their government. Yet China was arming U.S. enemies in Vietnam and was still in the throes of a domestic cultural revolution, a far more brutal crackdown than anything Iran's government has unleashed.

Assuming victory in Iraq, the U.S. rejected an authoritative Iranian offer for talks in May 2003 on all the issues dividing the two countries.

Iran's political system is more flexible than most Americans realize. A supporter of negotiations with the United

States, former president Akbar Hashemi Rafsanjani, has just been elected head of the body that can remove Iran's supreme religious leader and will choose his successor. Domestic opposition to Ahmadinejad has been growing, primarily because of his economic mismanagement. A genuine U.S. offer to talk could disarm him and other Iranian neoconservatives. A U.S. attack, on the other hand, would rally Iranians behind Ahmadinejad and boost his chances for re-election in 2009. U.S. bombing would provide a pretext for more repression and convince ordinary Iranians that the United States is indeed "the Great Satan," indifferent to the loss of Iranian lives and determined to prevent Iran from holding a position of influence in the Middle East.

13

A Military Response to Iran's Nuclear and Terrorist Threat Is Justified

Sean Rayment

Sean Rayment has written for many newspapers and is currently the defence and security correspondent of the Sunday Telegraph. *He is the author of* Into the Killing Zone: Dispatches from the Frontline in Afghanistan.

Iran has been involved in countless attacks against British soldiers in southern Iraq, and is thought to be behind the perfection of deadly improvised explosive devices (IEDs). Furthermore, its insistence on building a nuclear program that could lead to the manufacturing of atomic bombs threatens the security of the region and the interests of Great Britain and the United States. Military action against Iran might be justified.

It is, without doubt, responsible for the deaths and serious injuries of many British personnel, who have been attempting to contain the violence in southern Iraq.

The Islamic state's malignant involvement in its neighbour's internal strife escalated dramatically in April 2004 following the first uprising across Iraq by disaffected Shia militiamen.

As Iraq descended into murderous anarchy, Iran began channelling vast amounts of cash and weaponry to the burgeoning insurgency. Tehran, it seemed, was happy to fund any Shia militia group, providing it attacked the British and Americans, and therefore further destabilised Iraq.

The chaos that ensued allowed Iran to manoeuvre itself into the position of regional power broker, and fed Tehran's determination to become a nuclear power.

Iran's powerful Revolutionary Guards Force, known as the al-Quds, which is believed to be beyond the control of the central government, supported the Jaish al-Mahdi, or Mahdi Army, the Shia militia created by Moqtada al-Sadr, and the Badr Brigades—two groups whose hatred for the coalition was matched only by that for each other.

Tehran, it seemed, was happy to fund any Shia militia group, providing it attacked the British and Americans, and therefore further destabilised Iraq.

The cash was used to pay recruits—mainly young, unemployed and ill-educated Shia men from the slums of Baghdad and Basra—who were only too willing to take up arms against a force they regarded as occupiers rather than liberators.

It is also widely believed that the al-Quds perfected the improvised explosive devices (IED) which, in just a few short months, went from being rudimentary and unreliable to highly sophisticated lethal weapons capable of firing multiple projectiles and penetrating the armour of American and British tanks.

The IED, with its highly advanced infra-red triggering devices, became the weapon of choice for the insurgents and the technology was soon being passed to the Sunni and al-Qa'eda groups in Baghdad, who shared the same enemy, despite being locked in their own internal conflict.

As the American and British body counts increased so did the rhetoric from London and Washington. Both governments warned Iran to stay out of Iraq's affairs but each accusation was met with persistent denial by President Mahmoud Ahmadinejad, whose stock response became "where is the proof?"

But with a named British officer stating in a military report what many in the Army have suspected for years—Iran's direct involvement in the deaths of British troops—the question now is what does this mean for the Islamic Republic?

Iran's nuclear ambitions are completely unacceptable to both America and Britain, who now regard Iran's nuclear strategy as a one of the most dangerous threats, second only to Islamic terrorism, facing the West.

Even if the British Government wanted to exact some form of military revenge from Iran it is doubtful whether it has the capability. A one-off air strike would do little apart from enraging the pro-Iranian militias operating in southern Iraq.

Instead, it will add to the growing weight of evidence being accumulated by MI6 and the CIA that will one day be used to justify a limited but precise US-led attack against Tehran if it continues to develop nuclear weapons.

Iran's nuclear ambitions are completely unacceptable to both America and Britain, who now regard Iran's nuclear strategy as a one of the most dangerous threats, second only to Islamic terrorism, facing the West.

It has long been rumoured, but always officially denied that, given the right circumstances, Britain would support a limited air campaign against Iran's nuclear installations, such as the one launched by Israel in 1981 against the Iraqi Osirak nuclear reactor.

Although Britain is unlikely to take part in the attack itself, it would offer some form of support, such as in-flight refuelling or allowing the RAF's Airborne Warning and Control (AWAC) aircraft to be used.

Iran has been playing a dangerous game for too long. If it continues to do so it is highly likely the West will act—and with some justification, the relations of Britain's dead soldiers might say.

Is Tehran Responsible for These Deaths?

2nd Lt Joanna Yorke Dyer, who was a member of the Intelligence Corps, was killed in Basra in the early hours of April 5 2007, when the armoured vehicle in which she was travelling was destroyed by an improvised explosive device.

2nd Lt Dyer, who had trained with Prince William at Sandhurst Royal Military Academy, and three other soldiers were killed instantly, and the bomb left a 3ft crater in the road. The 24-year-old Oxford graduate, who was single and from Yeovil, had been in Iraq for just a few weeks.

Ft Lt Sarah-Jayne Mulvihill, 32, who was married and from Canterbury, Kent, was one of five Service personnel killed when a Royal Navy Lynx helicopter was hit by a missile fired by insurgents in Basra in May 2006.

The attack was one of the largest losses of life in a single incident in the entire war and was the first time a British helicopter had been shot down. An investigation later found that the missile which struck the aircraft originated from Iran.

Kingsman Alex Green, 21, from Warrington, Lancashire, was shot dead by an Iraqi gunman—dubbed the Basra sniper—in January 2007. Kingsman Green was serving with Chindit Company, based at the Old State Building, in the centre of Basra, at the time of his death.

He was part of a patrol that had earlier been escorting a convoy out of the city when he was ambushed. Although he was not killed outright, he died of his injuries later the same day. He was one of several British soldiers killed by the Basra sniper.

Cpl John Rigby, who was a member of the 4th Battalion The Rifles, was killed in a roadside bomb attack in June 2007.

The 24-year-old soldier, from Rye in East Sussex, died with his twin brother—who was also a soldier in the same regiment—by his side at the British field hospital in Basra.

His commanding officer, Lt Col Patrick Sanders, paid the following tribute to him: "He was a warrior—tough and fierce, swift and bold. And he was an astonishingly dedicated and charismatic leader. Like all the best soldiers, he inspired love, devotion and fierce loyalty in his men. They idolised him and would follow him anywhere."

14

Israel Might Have to Face the Iranian Threat Alone

Calev Ben-David

Calev Ben-David is a journalist for the Jerusalem Post.

Even though America understands the threat Iran is posing to the Middle East in general, and to Israel in particular, it has no interest in committing to yet another war. Israel, whose existence is gravely endangered by Iran's nuclear program, might have to act against America's wishes and attack Iran on its own.

"**I** know that your blood and your lives are at stake. Our blood and our lives are at stake in many places and may be in others. I think it is a necessity that Israel should never make itself seem responsible in the eyes of America and the world for making war. Israel will not be alone, unless it decides to go it alone."

So said [President] Lyndon Baines Johnson in a dramatic Oval Office meeting with then-Israeli foreign minister Abba Eban, just ten days before the outbreak of the 1967 war. Johnson was making a plea to Israel to give multi-lateral diplomacy one last chance to break Egypt's closure of the Straits of Tiran, and force it and Syria to back down on threats to drive the Israelis into the sea.

There was much at stake in that explosive situation—arguably, even more so than the current one between Israel, the US and Iran over the latter's nuclear program. The Soviet

Union was a staunch ally of Jerusalem's Arab enemies back then, and there was real concern that a military response by Israel could spread beyond a regional conflict into a potential superpower confrontation.

Echoes of the Cold War

Although an Israeli strike on Iranian nuclear facilities and Teheran's possible retaliation would likely have a global impact, 2008 is not 1967 and such Cold War scenarios are no longer relevant. But there are some significant ways in which the echoes of that period do reverberate in the standoff over the Iranian nuclear threat, including the potential strains it could introduce into the strategic relationship between Washington and Iran.

A direct link between the two popped up the past few days [in July 2008] with reports that during the discussions held here last week between Israeli military commanders and Admiral Michael Mullen, US Chairman of the Joint Chiefs of Staff, the inadvertent Israeli Air Force attack on the USS *Liberty* during the '67 war was cited as the type of incident that needed to be avoided in any future military actions in the region.

Although an Israeli strike on Iranian nuclear facilities and Teheran's possible retaliation would likely have a global impact, 2008 is not 1967 and such Cold War scenarios are no longer relevant.

Mullen has already gone on record as among those top American officials not only opposed to a US military response to the Iranian threat, but expressing concern over a unilateral Israeli response, telling the press last week he was concerned that the repercussions could open up a "third front" for US forces already strained by their missions in Iraq and Afghanistan.

Four decades ago, the American military was also over-stretched by its faltering war in Vietnam, and similar worries vexed Washington over being dragged into a conflict between Israel and its Arab enemies. The big difference, though, is that despite the isolated *Liberty* incident, the US did not have significant forces in the immediate area, as it does today in Iraq and the Persian Gulf.

The Fear of War

That [presence] not only raises the ante of possible American involvement (and casualties) in connection with an Israeli security operation; US military control of Iraqi airspace may require from Jerusalem greater coordination with—and approval from—Washington in advance of such action than at any time in the past.

There is an irony here worth noting; some critics of the Iraq War have emphasized the benefits to Israeli security accrued by the removal of Saddam Hussein's regime as a supposed leading motivation for supporters of the invasion, especially among Jewish neo-conservatives.

But many Israeli security and governmental officials, while certainly welcoming Saddam's downfall, were always more cautious and skeptical about a venture that involved a long-term commitment of direct American military involvement in the region, especially the extended stationing of US troops on Arab soil as part of a supposed effort in democratic nation-building.

The complications of that situation are now abundantly clear in the face-off over the Iranian nuclear threat, to the extent of it possibly limiting an Israeli response to a potential existential threat. Some security pundits are even asserting that given concerns in the American military establishment about a possible "third front," and Jerusalem's desire to do nothing that would endanger its crucial strategic relationship with the US, Israel will not act against Iran until obtaining explicit approval from Washington, or will rush its timetable in the belief that the best time to obtain that green light is while George W. Bush is still in office.

Israel has acted more than once against Washington's express wishes when it perceived it necessary to defend its essential security interests.

The Need to Protect Israel

There are sound reasons to accept that scenario, as well as historical precedent—unfortunately, not all of it positive from the Israeli perspective. Similar considerations were part of the reason Israel failed to launch a pre-emptive strike on Egyptian and Syrian forces in 1973, a precedent that still haunts Israeli policymakers.

Yet the premise that Washington has—or even wants—straight-up veto power over the Israeli response to the Iranian threat, or that Jerusalem would cede [grant] it, is a gross simplification of a more complex reality, both past and present.

As in '67, the bombing of the Iraqi Osirak reactor in 1981 and numerous other incidents, Israel has acted more than once against Washington's express wishes when it perceived it necessary to defend its essential security interests (and vice versa, needless to add).

But such tactical disagreements have never done more than temporary damage to the strategic US-Israeli relationship, because it is based not on short-term diplomatic interests, but on basic political, geo-political, historical and cultural links between the two nations. So it will ultimately be with the Iranian situation, despite fears of a "third front," a steep rise in the price of oil, or a temporary upsurge in terrorism.

The route of diplomatic efforts and economic sanctions against Teheran will play itself out in the coming year, resulting in either success or failure. At the end of that day, though, a day that increasingly cannot be too long in coming, if Israel has to act alone to protect itself it will do so—but only because once again, the world has left it alone.

Organizations to Contact

The editors have compiled the following list of organizations concerned with the issues debated in this book. The descriptions are derived from materials provided by the organizations. All have publications or information available for interested readers. The list was compiled on the date of publication of the present volume; the information provided here may change. Be aware that many organizations take several weeks or longer to respond to inquiries, so allow as much time as possible.

American-Iranian Council (AIC)

29A Wiggins Street, Princeton, NJ   08540
(609) 252-9099 • fax: (609) 252-9698
Web site: www.american-iranian.org

The AIC organizes and promotes the Iranian-American community and encourages its participation in the efforts for a more democratic, transparent, mutually respectful, and sustainable relationship between the United States and Iran. It provides books and articles for downloading on its extensive Web site.

Americans for Middle East Understanding (AMEU)

475 Riverside Drive, Room 245, New York, NY   10115-0245
(212) 870-2053 • fax: (212) 870-2050
e-mail: info@ameu.org
Web site: www.ameu.org

AMEU's purpose is to foster a better understanding in America of the history, goals, and values of Middle Eastern cultures and peoples, the rights of Palestinians, and the forces shaping U.S. policy in the Middle East. AMEU publishes *The Link*, a regular newsletter, as well as books and pamphlets on the Middle East.

The Brookings Institute
1775 Massachusetts Ave. NW, Washington, DC 20036
(202) 797-6000 • fax: (202) 797-6004
e-mail: brookinfo@brook.edu
Web site: www.brookings.org

The Brookings Institute is a think tank conducting research and education in foreign policy, economics, government, and the social sciences. Publications include the periodic *Policy Briefs* and books including *Terrorism and U.S. Foreign Policy*.

Center for Defense Information (CDI)
1779 Massachusetts Ave. NW, Suite 615
Washington, DC 20036-2109
(202) 332-0600 • fax: (202) 462-4559
e-mail: info@cdi.org
Web site: www.cdi.org

CDI is a nonpartisan, nonprofit organization that researches all aspects of global security. It seeks to educate the public and policy makers about weapons systems, security policy, and defense budgeting. It publishes the regular *Defense Monitor*.

Center for Strategic and International Studies (CSIS)
1800 K Street NW, Suite 400, Washington, DC 20006
(202) 887-0200 • fax: (202) 775-3199
Web site: www.csis.org

The center works to provide world leaders with strategic insights and policy options on current and emerging global issues. It publishes the *Washington Quarterly*, a journal on political, economic, and security issues, and other publications that can be downloaded from its Web site.

Central Intelligence Agency (CIA)
Office of Public Affairs, Washington, DC 20505
(703) 482-0623 • fax: (703) 482-1739
Web site: www.cia.gov

The Central Intelligence Agency was created in 1947 with the signing of the National Security Act by President Harry S. Truman. The CIA seeks to collect and evaluate intelligence related to the national security and provide appropriate dissemination of such intelligence. Publications such as the *Factbook on Intelligence*, are available on its Web site.

Foreign Policy Association (FPA)

470 Park Ave. South, New York, NY   10016
(212) 481-8100 • fax: (212) 481-9275
e-mail: info@fpa.org
Web site: www.fpa.org

The FPA is a nonprofit organization seeking to inspire the American public to learn more about the world. The FPA serves as a catalyst for developing awareness, understanding of, and providing informed opinions on global issues. It publishes the *Great Decisions* DVD series, and makes articles and discussions available online.

The Heritage Foundation

214 Massachusetts Ave. NE, Washington, DC   20002-4999
(202) 546-4400 • fax: (202) 546-8328
e-mail: info@heritage.org
Web site: www.heritage.org

Founded in 1973, The Heritage Foundation is a research and educational institute whose mission is to formulate and promote conservative public policies based on the principles of free enterprise, limited government, individual freedom, and a strong national defense. It publishes many books on foreign policy, such as *Winning the Long War*.

Institute for Policy Studies (IPS)

1112 16th Street NW, Suite 600, Washington, DC   20036
(202) 234-9382 • fax: (202) 387-7915
Web site: www.ips-dc.org

The IPS is a progressive think tank working to develop societies built around the values of justice and nonviolence. It has published reports including *Global Perspectives: A Media Guide to Foreign Policy Experts*. Articles are also available online.

Middle East Media Research Institute (MEMRI)
PO Box 27837, Washington, DC   20038-7837
(202) 955-9070 • fax: (202) 955-9077
e-mail: memri@memri.org
Web site: www.memri.org

MEMRI translates and disseminates articles and commentaries from Middle East media sources and provides original research and analysis on the region. Its Jihad and Terrorism Studies Project monitors radical Islamist groups and individuals and their reactions to acts of terrorism around the world.

National Iranian American Council (NIAC)
1411 K Street NW, Suite 600, Washington, DC   20005
(202) 386-6325 • fax: (202) 386-6409
Web site: www.niacouncil.org

The National Iranian American Council is a nonpartisan, nonprofit organization dedicated to advancing the interests of the Iranian-American community. It helps supply the resources, knowledge, and tools to enable greater civic participation by Iranian Americans and informed decision making by lawmakers. The NIAC provides articles on U.S.-Iran relations on its Web site.

National Security Agency (NSA)
9800 Savage Road, Fort Meade, MD   20755-6248
(301) 688-6524
Web site: www.nsa.gov

The NSA coordinates, directs, and performs activities, such as designing cipher systems, that protect American information systems and produce foreign intelligence information. Speeches, briefings, and reports are available online.

Bibliography

Books

Yonah Alexander
and Milton
Hoenig

*The New Iranian Leadership:
Ahmadinejad, Terrorism, Nuclear
Ambition, and the Middle East.*
Westport, CT: Greenwood Publishing
Group, 2007.

Ali Ansari

*Confronting Iran: The Failure of
American Foreign Policy and the Next
Great Crisis in the Middle East.* New
York: Basic Books, 2006.

Ali Ansari

Iran Under Ahmadinejad. New York:
Routledge, 2008.

Touraj Atabaki,
ed.,

*The State and the Subaltern:
Modernization, Society and the State
in Turkey and Iran.* London, UK: I.B.
Tauris, 2007.

Lois Beck and
Guity Nashat, eds.

*Women in Iran from 1800 to the
Islamic Republic.* Champaign:
University of Illinois Press, 2004.

Ilan Berman

*Tehran Rising: Iran's Challenge to the
United States.* Lanham, MD: Rowman
& Littlefield, 2005.

Daniel Brumberg

*Reinventing Khomeini: The Struggle
for Reform in Iran.* Chicago:
University of Chicago Press, 2001.

Shahram Chubin   *Iran's Nuclear Ambitions.* Washington, DC: Carnegie Endowment for International Peace, 2006.

Anthony Cordesman   *Iran's Developing Military Capabilities.* Washington, DC: Center for Strategic and International Studies Press, 2005.

Anthony Cordesman   *The Military Balance in the Middle East.* Westport, CT: Praeger, 2004.

Anthony Cordesman and Khalid Al-Rodhan   *Gulf Military Forces in an Era of Asymmetric Wars.* Westport, CT: Praeger Security International, 2007.

Mike Evans and Jerome Corsi   *Showdown with Nuclear Iran: Radical Islam's Messianic Mission to Destroy Israel and Cripple the United States.* Nashville, TN: Nelson Current, 2006.

Mark Hitchcock   *The Apocalypse of Ahmadinejad: The Revelation of Iran's Nuclear Prophet.* Portland, OR: Multnomah Publications, 2007.

Alireza Jafarzadeh   *The Iran Threat: President Ahmadinejad and the Coming Nuclear Crisis.* New York: Palgrave Macmillan, 2007.

Masoud Kazemzadeh   *Islamic Fundamentalism, Feminism, and Gender Inequality in Iran Under Khomeini.* Lanham, MD: University Press of America, 2002.

Nikki R. Keddie   *Modern Iran: Roots and Results of Revolution.* New Haven: Yale University Press, 2006.

Christin   *Iran's Persian Gulf Policy: From*
Marschall   *Khomeini to Khatami.* New York:
                          Routledge, 2003.

Yossi Melman and   *The Nuclear Sphinx of Tehran:*
Meir Javedanfar   *Mahmoud Ahmadinejad and the State*
                          of Iran. New York: Basic Books, 2008.

Kasra Naji   *Ahmadinejad: The Secret History of*
                          Iran's Radical Leader. Berkeley, CA:
                          University of California Press, 2008.

Kenneth Pollack   *The Persian Puzzle: The Conflict*
                          Between Iran and America. New York:
                          Random House, 2005.

James Russell   *Proliferation of Weapons of Mass*
                          Destruction in the Middle East:
                          Directions and Policy Options in the
                          New Century. New York: Palgrave
                          Macmillan, 2006.

Richard Russell   *Weapons Proliferation and War in the*
                          Greater Middle East: Strategic Contest.
                          New York: Routledge, 2005.

Milton Schwartz,   *Iran: Political Issues, Nuclear*
ed.   *Capabilities, and Missile Range.* New
                          York: Nova Science Publishers, 2006.

Elaine Sciolino   *Persian Mirrors: The Elusive Face of*
                          Iran. New York: Simon and Schuster,
                          2001.

Henry Sokolowski   *Getting Ready for a Nuclear-Ready*
and Patrick   *Iran.* Carlisle Barracks, PA: Strategic
Clawson, eds.   Studies Institute, U.S. Army War
                          College, 2005.

Kenneth Timmerman	*Countdown to Crisis: The Coming Nuclear Showdown with Iran.* New York: Crown Forum, 2005.
Al Venter	*Iran's Nuclear Option: Tehran's Quest for the Atom Bomb.* Philadelphia, PA: Casemate, 2005.

Periodicals

Iason Athanasiadis	"A Saffron Revolution in Iran?" *Jane's Islamic Affairs Analyst*, January 2008.
Ash Bali	"The US and the Iranian Nuclear Impasse," *Middle East Report*, Winter 2006.
Jack Boureston and Charles Ferguson	"Assessing Iran's Plutonium Reprocessing Capabilities," *Jane's Intelligence Review*, March 2004.
Jack Boureston and Charles Ferguson	"Iranian Research Indicates Pursuit of Nuclear Enrichment Technology," *Jane's Intelligence Review*, May 2006.
Wyn Bowen and Joanna Kidd	"The Iranian Nuclear Challenge," *International Affairs*, March 2004.
Peter Brookes	"Iran Emboldened: Tehran Seeks to Dominate Middle East Politics," *Armed Forces Journal*, April 2007.
John Calabrese	"Renewing Iran-Pakistan Relations," *Jane's Islamic Affairs Analyst*, May 2008.

Patrick Clawson "The Islamic Republic's Economic Failure," *Middle East Quarterly*, Fall 2008.

Gregory Copley "Ahmadi-Nejad's 'Message' Reflects Belief that Tehran Has the Strategic Initiative," *Defense & Foreign Affairs Strategic Policy*, 2006.

Gregory Copley "Iran's Plan for a Lebanese Civil War Is Integral to a Broader Strategy," *Defense & Foreign Affairs Strategic Policy*, 2006.

Anthony Cordesman "Iran and the United States: The Nuclear Issue," *Middle East Policy*, Spring 2008.

Adel Darwish "Iran Flexes Its Muscles: Iran Has a Grand Plan to Become One of the Most Influential Countries in the Region. Was the Arrest of 15 British Forces Personnel in Disputed Waters During March Part of This Scheme?" *The Middle East*, May 2007.

James Devine and Julian Schofield "Coercive Counter-Proliferation and Escalation: Assessing the Iran Military Option," *Defense & Security Analysis*, June 2006.

Manochehr Dorraj and Carrie Currier "Lubricated with Oil: Iran-China Relations in a Changing World," *Middle East Policy*, Summer 2008.

Kaveh Ehsani "Iran: The Populist Threat to Democracy," *Middle East Report*, Winter 2006.

Steven Ekovich   "Iran and New Threats in the Persian
                     Gulf and Middle East," *Orbis: A
                     Journal of World Affairs*, Winter 2004.

Charles Ferguson   "The Four Faces of Nuclear
                     Terrorism," *Naval War College
                     Review*, Spring 2005.

Mark Fitzpatrick   "Assessing Iran's Nuclear
                     Programme," *Survival*, Fall 2006.

Reuel Marc   "Countering Iran," *Weekly Standard*,
Gerecht   May 19, 2008.

Matt Hilburn   "Asymmetric Strategy: Growing
                     Iranian Navy Relies on 'Unbalanced
                     Warfare' Tactics," *Seapower*,
                     December 2006.

Robin Hughes   "Briefing: Iran's Ballistic Missile
                     Developments," *Jane's Defence Weekly*,
                     September 13, 2006.

Michael Jacobson   "Sanctions Against Iran: A Promising
                     Struggle," *Washington Quarterly*,
                     Summer 2008.

Reuben Johnson   "Iran Strives for Self-Sufficiency in
                     Conventional Weapons," *Jane's
                     Intelligence Review*, December 2006.

Riad Kahwaji and   "U.S. Seeks Arab Allies Against Iran,"
Barbara   *Defense News*, October 16, 2006.
Opall-Rome

Richard Kauffman   "Inside Iran: First-Person
                     Encounters," *The Christian Century*,
                     June 17, 2008.

Paul Melly

"Tehran's Global Gas Ambitions,"
MEED: Middle East Economic Digest,
June 27, 2008.

Gary Milhollin
and Valerie Lincy

"Iran's Nuclear Card," *Commentary*,
February 2004.

Fariborz
Mokhtari

"Mahmud Ahamadinejad's
Presidency: What Does Iran Really
Want?" *American Foreign Policy
Interests*, October 2006.

Michael Oren

"Israel's Truce with Hamas Is a
Victory for Iran," *Wall Street Journal*,
June 19, 2008.

Richard Russell

"Iran in Iraq's Shadow: Dealing with
Tehran's Nuclear Weapons Bid,"
Parameters, Fall 2004.

Amin Saikal

"The Iran Nuclear Dispute,"
*Australian Journal of International
Affairs*, June 2006.

Abbas William
Samii

"The Iranian Nuclear Issue and
Informal Networks," *Naval War
College Review*, Winter 2006.

Paul Starobin

"Of Mullahs and MADness," *National
Journal*, May 20, 2006.

Ray Takeyh

"The Iran Puzzle: The Islamic
Republic Is the Most Troublesome
Mideast State, but Has Signaled Its
Desire to Deal with Us. How Should
America Respond to Iran?" *The
American Prospect*, May 22, 2007.

Adam Tarock   "Iran's Nuclear Programme and the West," *Third World Quarterly*, June 2006.

Alex Vatanka   "Turkmenistan's Cold Surprise for Iran," *Jane's Islamic Affairs Analyst*, April 2008.

Al Venter   "Iran's Nuclear Option," *Soldier of Fortune*, May 2005.

Index

V

Vietnam, 95, 104
The Volunteer (Ross), 61–62

W

Walsh, Jim, 68–81
William, Prince of Wales, 100
World War III, 82

World War IV, 82, 86

Y

Yaari, Ehud, 11–12
Young, Michael, 13

Z

Zhou Enlai, 95
Zunes, Stephen, 14–21